AROUND
THE WORLD
in 500 Days

AROUND THE WORLD
in 500 Days

*The circumnavigation
of the merchant bark
Charles Stewart, 1883-1884,
recounted with zest and detail
by the captain's daughter,
Hattie Atwood Freeman*

Edited by Curtis Dahl

MYSTIC SEAPORT • MYSTIC, CONNECTICUT, 1999

Many years ago, during my first voyage, I witnessed a sunset singularly impressive, while sailing the Mediterranean sea. Our bark seemed to feel the spirit of night, and impelled by a light breeze sailed towards her port of destination.

The sun going down in a blaze of splendor, converted the expanse of sea and sky dotted with clouds into one mass of molten rainbow. I reached out my hands to such ethereal splendor.

And now at the sunset and eventide of my good Father's life, I write this book. My thoughts turning with special tenderness to all the friends herein mentioned who helped make these voyages a lasting happiness and pleasure; and tonight I long to know how and where each and every one is and would gladly reach out my hands once more in welcome.

H. A. F.
Norton, Massachusetts, April 26, 1907[G]

Hattie Atwood Freeman (from the original book)

The bark 'Charles Stewart' as depicted by the stowaway artist Charles
Bieri, a painting now owned by Marion L. Norman and reproduced
here with her permission. (photo: MSM 92-17-30A).

N

HATTIE ATWOOD'S
TRIP AROUND THE WORLD
1883 - 1884

0°

BRISBANE

HOBART, TASMANIA

Mystic Seaport
75 Greenmanville Avenue
Mystic, CT 06355

©1999 by Mystic Seaport Museum, Inc.

Cataloging in Publication data:

Freeman, Hattie Atwood.
  Around the world in 500 days : the circumnavigation of the merchant bark Charles
Stewart, 1883-1884, recounted with zest and detail by the captain's daughter, Hattie Atwood
Freeman / edited by Curtis Dahl, — Mystic, Conn. : Mystic Seaport, 1999.
  p. : ill., maps ; cm.
  Originally published: A trip around the world on board the merchantman bark "Charles
Stewart" of New York. 1907.
  Includes bibliographical references and glossary.

  1. Freeman, Hattie Atwood. 2. Charles Stewart (Bark) 3. Voyages around the world. 4.
Seafaring life. 5. Women and the sea. I. Dahl, Curtis. II. Title. III. Title: A trip around the world.

G440.F73 1999

ISBN 0-913372-90-0

Book and cover design by Caroline Rowntree, New Paltz, New York
Illustrations for chapter openings by Paul Rowntree

Table of Contents

EDITOR'S PREFACE

14

ACKNOWLEDGEMENTS

17

A NOTE ON THE EDITING

20

Chapter One: PREPARATION

23

Chapter Two: NEW YORK

29

Chapter Three: AT SEA

33

Chapter Four: MEALS AT SEA

37

Chapter Five: AT SEA

40

Chapter Six: HOBART, TASMANIA

49

Chapter Seven: LEAVING HOBART FOR BRISBANE

56

Chapter Eight: BRISBANE

59

Chapter Nine: ONCE MORE AT SEA

66

Chapter Ten: VALPARAISO

69

Chapter Eleven: LOBOS DE AFUERAG

74

Chapter Twelve: AWAY FOR GIBRALTAR
81
Chapter Thirteen: ONWARD WE GO
85
Chapter Fourteen: GIBRALTAR
89
Chapter Fifteen: BARCELONA
98
Chapter Sixteen: POND SAILING AND TRAPANI
113
Chapter Seventeen: HOMEWARD BOUND
130
EPILOGUE
139

Background and Notes: glossary of persons, places,
maritime terms, and allusions
143
List of vessels met by the *Charles Stewart*
or mentioned in Background and Notes
199
Appendix I: Summary of the Meteorological
Log of Hattie Atwood's 1884-1885 voyage
to Messina, Sicily, and return
203
Appendix II: Captain Atwood's
"Thousand-Mile Race on a Floating Volcano"
205

PREFACE

Hattie Atwood Freeman's account of her voyage around the world in 1883-84 in a tramp merchant bark is a vivid record of sea life as seen by a girl of 17. She makes us feel the excitement of storms and danger, the dullness of long weeks in the Pacific without sight of land, the pleasure of arrivals into such colorful ports as Hobart, Brisbane, Gibraltar, Valparaiso, Barcelona, and the guano islands off the coast of Peru.

But to an even greater degree it is Hattie's own personality that makes the book so attractive. From the very first page, where she describes herself as the ugly duckling of her large family—none of her sisters wished to go in the *Charles Stewart* because their thoughts were on romance and marriage—her wry humor, her amusing self-deprecation, her sense of adventure, her enjoyment of life, and her capability to meet any situation, make this deftly written account a pleasure to read. Hattie was far more than a mere passenger on the bark. In a brief time she became an accomplished seawoman able to navigate, keep the meteorological log, and mind the chart while the vessel sailed at night up a crooked and dangerous river. She kept the ship's accounts, she was a good companion to her father, she got on well with the crew, and she delighted in the people she met and the scenes she saw when in port.

The book also has historical importance. It records a social phenomenon rarely so clearly depicted elsewhere. Many captains of American, British, and European merchant vessels brought with them to sea their wives and daughters. Wherever a number of vessels gathered in any port of call, a merry social whirl of visiting, partying, sightseeing, flirting, and shopping immediately developed. The vessels in any one port came and went, but other vessels took their places, and so the port's sea society continued. As a young single woman of 17 Hattie was obviously at the center of such social activity. She flirted with a young Italian in Trapani, explored Barcelona with the mate, chased a visiting captain around the cabin with a fork to steal from him a piece of chicken, organized an evening of singing on board the *Charles Stewart*, and had herself rowed from ship to ship to make courtesy calls. Parties and sightseeing trips were fun after long weeks at sea, and Hattie's good humor, vigor, and outgoing personality made her just the girl to enliven and enjoy them.

Curtis Dahl

A Trip Around the World

ON BOARD THE MERCHANTMAN BARK "CHARLES STEWART" OF NEW YORK

BY
HATTIE ATWOOD FREEMAN
1907

Original title page of 'A Trip Around the World'

ACKNOWLEDGEMENTS

In the preparation of this edition I have incurred many debts both to individuals and institutions. President George Yelle of the Norton Historical Society first brought to my attention Hattie Atwood Freeman's *A Trip Around the World,* a copy of which is in the Society's collections. Harry Burbank of Norton did extensive research for me in Maine and Massachusetts census records. When I could not trace where Hattie had lived after her husband's death, Richard Charette provided the key by finding the date of her death on her grave in the Norton Common Cemetery. Benny Keene, Sr., who remembers as a boy having seen old Edgar Freeman on Memorial Day, explained and differentiated the three different Freeman families of Chartley. In my research in Maine I benefited greatly from the resources of the Maine Historical Society, the Maine Maritime Museum, the Penobscot Marine Museum, the Maine State Archives, and the Maine State Library. Christy Coombs of the Bangor Public Library has been tireless in answering questions. She referred me to a skilled local historian of Bangor, James B. Vickery, who generously provided needed pictures and facts. Equally important has been the help of Katherine Trickey, Nadine Hoyt, and other members of the Hampden (Maine) Historical Society.

This volume would not have come to publication without the initial enthusiastic support of Jerry Morris, then librarian and director of publications at Mystic Seaport. [His successors, Andy German and Joe Gribbins, with efficiency, good humor, and great skill have brought the book to completion.] Reference librarian Paul O'Pecko and associate curator Philip Budlong have helped greatly with facts and pictures. My friend Stuart Frank, director of the Kendall Whaling Museum, has given advice and encouragement enthusiastically and unstintingly; he was always there to help when needed.

In searching for pictures and information relevant to the *Charles Stewart*'s stays at Hobart and Brisbane I have been assisted with particular imagination and assiduity by Tony Marshall of the State Library of Tasmania and C. G. Sheehan of the John Oxley Library in Queensland. Both have gone far beyond the call of duty. So too has William Kooiman of the Reference Department of the Library of the National Maritime Museum in San Francisco, who provided needed information on the vessels of which Captain Horace Atwood was at various times master. I owe even more to the diligent and imaginative assistance of T. Lane Moore of the Civil Reference Branch of the National Archives. Tirelessly and patiently he came up with important documents relative to the *Charles Stewart*'s 1883-84 voyage that I would never have known existed. Curators and librarians at the Peabody Essex Museum, the Wheaton College Library, the Boston Athenaeum, the Society for the Preservation of New England Antiquities, the Steamship Historical Society, the Museum of the City of New York, the Belfast (Maine) Public Library, the Mariners' Museum in Newport News, the several museums and libraries of Newburyport and Old Newburyport, and numerous other libraries and museums, have also contributed generously. Professors Briton Busch of Colgate University and Roberto Ruiz of Wheaton College have helped with their special knowledge, as has Joan Druett of New Zealand, editor of *"She Was a Sister Sailor": The Whaling Journals of Mary Brewster,* published by Mystic Seaport.

Fairly late in my research, with great good fortune I located members of the Atwood and Freeman families, without whose contributions this edition would be much less interesting and vivid. Hattie Atwood's niece Henrietta Atwood Briggs, who knew her well, has contributed not only personal recollections but also two important newspaper articles on Captain Horace Atwood, one the account of his near-fatal voyage in a burning ice-ship (see Appendix II), the other on his life in Hampden after his retirement from the sea. Through the courtesy of Attorney Roy L. Smith, grandson of Hattie's stepson Charles Freeman, with whom she lived after her husband's death. I have with great pleasure come to know Eloise Valentine Freeman Smith and Marion L. Norman, respectively Charles's daughter and grandaughter. Both, of course, knew Hattie intimately; they still live within a block of Charles Freeman's house in Pawcatuck, Connecticut, in which Hattie lived for over two decades. They provided fascinating personal information about Hattie and what she was like and, to my great delight, showed me and allowed to be copied for this edition both a painting of the bark *Charles Stewart* by the stowaway Swiss artist Charles Bieri and the original of the photographic portrait of herself that Hattie had taken, as she records in the book, in Barcelona. To their interest, encouragement, friendliness, and generosity I owe very much.

I wish to thank also Marilyn Todesco of the Faculty Secretaries Office of Wheaton College for her cheerfulness and accuracy in doing much of the typing.

A NOTE ON THE EDITING

In editing *A Trip Around the World on Board the Merchantman Bark "Charles Stewart" of New York,* the book's 1907 title, a strong effort has been made to preserve as much as possible Hattie's own voice and to present the text of her volume as nearly as she wrote it. Hattie's misspellings, which definitely add to the charm and feel of her book, have generally been left uncorrected. In some instances when the errors clearly seem to be the printer's rather than the author's, or where they obscure the sense, spellings or words have been altered. Such emendations are indicated by square brackets.

In order to present Hattie's narrative in a form that can be read easily and quickly, and which reproduces the verve of the original, annotations and explanations have whenever possible been relegated to Background and Notes and to a Glossary and a List of Vessels, both alphabetically arranged. The first of these gives information about persons, places, allusions, and special maritime terms. The latter gives information on the vessels mentioned, whether in Hattie's book or in Backgrounds and Notes. A superscript "G" refers the reader to the Glossary. A superscript "V" refers the reader to the List of Vessels. The editor's hope is that the casual reader will be able to read the volume on pages uncluttered by footnotes and documentation, but that the more serious reader who wishes further information about Hattie, her father, the bark and other vessels, along with the places visited, can find it in the Background and Notes and these appendices. In either case, *A Trip Around the World* should be fun to read.

Excerpts from the official Meteorlogical Logs which

Hattie kept on both of her voyages have been included. They add bits of color and information that support and vivify her narrative, not that it needs anything like such help.

The daily occurrences on board a ship are marked on a board or slate, called a log-board or log-slate. The remarks made on the log-board are daily copied into a book called a Log Book. Some keep only an abstract; others keep a full copy.

The American Practical Navigator
by Nathaniel Bowditch[G]

*'I had a great desire
to accompany him on a trip
to Hobart, Tasmania'*

Chapter One

PREPARATION

My Father, Captain Horace Atwood of Hampden,[G] Maine, was a sea-captain in command of the bark *Charles Stewart*[G] hailing from New York. I had a great desire to accompany him on a trip to Hobart, Tasmania. The idea of taking a trip on the bark was first entertained by my two elder sisters, but when the destination of the bark was determined it meant so extended a trip they decided they could not be deprived so long of those tender affections that come to most young ladies of twenty and twenty-one years of age, thereupon they gave up the trip to remain near those affections. Now this had never been my happy lot, and when I have given a description of myself the reader will see the reason plainly. Imagine, if you can, a girl seventeen years and nine months old, five feet five inches high, weight one hundred pounds, dull expressionless blue eyes, brown hair painfully straight, large mouth, regular teeth, generous nose and ears, high cheek bones, loud full voice, unconquerable temper, and complexion (as her mother often told her) like a light colored Indian, and it will not need a magnifying glass or encyclopedia to understand why I had never received those tender affections from the opposite sex. Nevertheless I was not a bad girl at heart and had many friends among my schoolmates.

After considerable correspondence between my father and mother, who were in New York, and the owners of the vessel, it was decided that I was to take the trip, and a most delighted girl I was.

Riding on the steam cars and the novelty of packing a trunk for the first time were uppermost in my mind. I think here I will give a description of my clothes which are distinctly fresh in my memory, and after I have finished if you cannot see why I did not turn the heads of all eligible young men and crowned heads of foreign climes you must indeed be dead to all sense of attraction. My best dress for winter months was a gay plaid in red, green, yellow, blue, black. It was new and quite a pretty dress and I wore that dress five years to my certain knowledge, also a beaver coat and hat. Well I remember the long plume and bright bird that adorned that hat, a blue and velvet turban with blue tips, and a black chip hat of the previous summer. Sometime before my birth my father had bought my mother a Japanese silk dress, gray with fine black stripes in it, very suitable for a matron but hardly for a girl in her teens. This had been made over for me, quite a pretty dress and I felt as if "Queen Victory," as we girls used to say, could not have such a fine dress. This was adorned with a sash of shaded blue ribbon with red and black stripes through it that had previously done duty as bonnet strings to one of mother's bonnets, gay? Why, I was just dazzling as the darkey girls tell about. Next I remember, came what my father called my bed-ticking dress. It had previously belonged to my sister next older than I. This was a wood color with more stripes. A black bunting dress which had previously belonged to my oldest sister came in for a share of the trunk, a plum–colored skirt and several odd waists, all heirlooms, and let me say right here, if you are ever to be born again look out that you are not third on the list of arrivals so that you can have something new once in a while. Filling the trunk with all necessary articles and ribbons, shoes, underclothes I locked the lid down tight and on January twelve, eighteen hundred and eighty-three, I left my brothers and sisters in Maine and timidly started on a trip alone. I stayed with an aunt in Bangor all night and in the morning my uncle kindly put me on a train for Boston and away I go on my trip around the world. I arrived in Boston at four-thirty P.M., and as no one met me at the station I took a carriage and was drawn to the home of my father's sister, where I was cordially welcomed and told I had done the right thing, and felt like an experienced traveler. Three days in Boston where I saw many new and interesting sights. Large buildings seemed to impress me the most; up to that time I believe the Bangor House was the largest building I had ever seem. Horse cars with plenty of yellow straw in the bottom to keep the feet warm. My mother's sister Kate[G] took me to the Old State House and bought my ticket to

New York via the Fall River line.^G She took me into the large stores, out to lunch, to Child's Art rooms^G; she also bought me a diary and asked me to keep it, and it is from that diary that I am writing this book.

Leaving Boston by train for Fall River and thence by boat to New York. My! How it fretted me to think I might not be able to find the boat at Fall River, but after all my anxiety over the matter I stepped off the cars and nearly fell into the paddle box of the steamer.

I follow some ladies into the cabin and sit down on a red velvet chair, my stateroom key in my hand and my traveling bag by my side. After a while I asked a stewardess, as I afterwards found out, where my stateroom was and she kindly told me the door right side of me; again I felt like an experienced traveler to have chosen a red velvet chair so near my stateroom door. I went in and followed my aunt's directions: "If there is a lock and bolt on your stateroom door, use the bolt and not the lock."

I found the bolt and slipped it into place and wondered how I would find New York. I went to sleep and slept the night through, to wake up and find the boat not moving. I dressed myself, left the stateroom key, and for fear the boat would go back to Fall River with me on board, I went out on the pier and stood about watching for my father who was to meet me. After what seemed an eternity, I saw a man approaching me with a smile on his face and my aunt's advice once more came home to me.

"Look out for any man who tries to make advances to you, and if you want to ask any questions ask them of a woman or policeman."

So I look away from the man, but as he came nearer I saw that it was my own father; he had shaved off his moustache and that had changed him. He had been on the

South Street, near Cuyler's Alley, New York, 1887.
(Museum of the City of New York)

boat and could not find me; but now I was safe and he con-
ducted me across the city to South Street Pier Number Six,
pointing out as we went along: Trinity Church, Wall Street,
the Custom House, etc. At last we reach the bark. What a
funny sensation as I cross the gang plank and enter a door
that I had to stoop to pass through, into a cabin where I
found my mother, also the mate's wife[G] who was my Sunday
School teacher.

Thus I arrive so far on my journey.

Charles Stewart (Courtesy of James B. Vickery)

'I never dreamed there were so many fish in the seas...'

Chapter Two

NEW YORK

After the welcome was over and father had ordered me some breakfast, I had a chance to look around at what was to be my home for the next year at least. The cabin which extended the width of the house[G] was finished in light wood with flowers on each panel and highly polished, a sky-light overhead and two small windows, a hair-cloth lounge extending the length of the room on either side, camp chairs and small center table completed the furnishings of the room. On the wall a portrait of the gentleman the vessel was named for, a familiar face that was company many a day. My stateroom was just large enough to contain a bunk with two drawers beneath it and my trunk. It was just space for me to turn around. My father's stateroom was of comfortable size, double bunk, desk, clothes press, two windows, a small bathroom with generous tub; here we kept father's trunk and the two chronometers, a toilet room with medicine chest, a dining room with table that would seat seven, by "sitting fine," a small stove that has cooked many a good lunch, a cupboard on the starboard side, a storeroom on the port side. The storeroom had a sugar locker in it with a broad cover just high enough for a seat, and many an hour have I sat there reading and studying Spanish with the mate, who was a townsman of ours, Mr. Horace C. Whitmore,[G] so he seemed like our own folks. We were quite a happy family except when he and I would fight about some trifling matter concerning home affairs or people. A forward and after gangway,[G] a mate's and second mate's room, who was Mr. Florens, a Swede and a smart man, but could not pronounce "th," a lookout in the forward gangway where I have witnessed many a raging storm. This completed the cabin. A clean poop deck[G] and generous booby hatch,[G] where I walked many a mile and sat many an hour, a fine promenade on top of the house.[G] This was where I was supposed to pass my out of doors life, and many a storm and many a beautiful scene have I witnessed from that deck.

The scenes around New York piers were new, and many a queer sight have I seen while watching from the storm house window.

"Apple Mary,"[G] a queer character who sold fruit along the piers. Such clothes! Worse than mine. I felt that I was better dressed than I thought for. Pieces of boot legs tied onto her feet with rags served as shoes, ragged skirts and apron, a handkerchief over her head, and money in the bank. Afterwards I read of her death and she had over fifteen hundred dollars in the bank. She was known by all the seafaring men who patronized her. She was quite a novel sight to me, such apparent signs of poverty, but after a visit to Europe it was tame. Of beggars and cripples you will hear later.

While in New York I visited Central Park, Museum,ᴳ Cleopatra's Needle,ᴳ Art Rooms,ᴳ Greenwood Cemetery,ᴳ Castle Garden.ᴳ I heard the famous T. DeWitt Talmageᴳ preach twice, and it was the largest gathering of people I had ever seen. I remember one Sunday it was very dark and disagreeable outside and the last hymn "The morning light is breaking" was from the pen of my good friend Dr. Samuel F. Smith,ᴳ author of our national hymn. Just as the hymn was commenced the sun came out and filled the Tabernacle so bright, and such a change as came over the faces of that congregation. Brooklyn Bridge and Batholdi Statueᴳ were in course of construction.

A very interesting place is Castle Garden where the immigrants are landed, and Fulton Marketᴳ where I saw every kind of provision namable and unnamable. I never dreamed there were so many fish in the seas, let alone so many different kinds. The elevated railroad was a novelty and I used to enjoy riding so much. I visited all the large stores and saw many beautiful residences, this with the friends and callers, the strange way of doing work, visiting friends in Brooklyn, were all enjoyable and helped to pass the time quickly. The vessel had completed loading a general cargo, consisting of nearly every namable article from a shoe pegᴳ to carriages, pianos and organs, and everybody was busy getting the ship ready for sea, and on January twenty-ninth, eighteen hundred and eighty-three, the vessel was ready to sail.

Mother and Mrs. Whitmore were packing up ready to go home. I was all interest to see the sailors that were to work the vessel. They arrived on board at ten o'clock in the forenoon, seven young men, tall, short, thick, thin, one colored man called Bender and there were Billie, James, Mike, Tom, Henry, George, and to complete the list[G] of souls on board not only mentioned was John Samuels– "Ah Sam"–a Chinaman, who was steward and cook, a good fellow.

At half past twelve a carriage arrived to take mother and Mrs. Whitmore away, and I said goodbye. The tug boat came along side and work was commenced to get out to sea. I was so fascinated I did not half realize what was going on. We commence to creep out into the harbor and I remember the last familiar face I saw for eighteen months except those who were with me, was Capt. George Atwood,[G] a cousin of father's who had helped make New York very pleasant.

A fatherly pilot was on board and down the harbor and bay we crept and saw Governor's Island, Staten Island, the Hospital and Light Ships, Batholdi's Statue,[G] vessels and sailing craft of all descriptions. The motion of the vessel commenced to be disagreeable and I went below. When I appeared father said:

"Hattie you look white."

"I am sea sick." How the pilot laughed, but he was a good–natured fellow and spoke encouragingly and when he left the vessel for the tug I was ready to lay down my tired head and would have been glad to lay down my stomach also, but I am sure it came up. But I was one of the lucky ones and after six o'clock had no trouble if I kept my head down, and I went to sleep to awake at sea.

'Water, blue gloriously blue,
every wave with
a white bonnet on.'

Chapter Three

AT SEA

*T*uesday, January thirtieth. How I must have slept. The first thing I remember was my father saying: "Don't you want to go into your own bunk so I can lie down."

I had gone to sleep in my father's bed, it being on the lee side of the vessel, and he had been kept up all night by getting out to sea in squally weather.

He took me in his arms and carried me to my bed and although I felt weak I was not sick.

The mate and steward came and offered fruit and food but I was not in a hungry frame of stomach. I lay in my bed until four P. M. when my father brought a shawl and hat and said "I want you to look at something."

He took me up the after gangway.

How I wish I could describe the scene before me, but I can not. Yes, there are pictures, but never can a brush or human agency paint what I saw. Water, blue gloriously blue, every wave with a white bonnet on. Sky blue, gloriously blue! with silver white clouds dancing! yes, dancing all over it, and right astern chasing us, every bound seeming to say, I'll get you, came a brig, her sails so white, her hull so black and shiny! She seemed to be having the best time of her life, how she would come, it seemed as if I could touch her, and father said she was two miles away. But where was the land? Sky and wave touched and it was difficult to tell where one commenced and the other left off. But my first glimpse of the ocean can never be erased from my memory, and many a time have I closed my eyes and seen that wonderful sight that can never be expressed by word or brush. The English language with all its adjectives cannot do it. Only the realization, impressed upon the memory, can only show you the wonders and beauty of nature.

I stayed up about two hours, and then felt so weak and tired I went to bed, and father told me to take off my clothes and make myself as comfortable as possible.

The next day I was still weak, but father said I had better dress and move about, which I did for a couple of hours and went on deck. Did I see what I did the day before. No, the sky and sea were blue and vessels in company, but it was as nothing to the day before.

On February first my father came in the morning at seven o'clock and said:

"Hattie, If I were you I would get up this morning and dress."

I did so, and he took me down on the main deck and placed my arm in his and took me on a nice walk, back and forth, back and forth, until the breakfast bell rang and we went into breakfast. I ate quite a meal, and afterwards made the beds and mended a coat for father and read some; later father made me some beef tea which tasted nice and made me feel better and stronger.

In the cargo was a consignment of organs to a Brisbane firm and only five could be placed in the hold of the vessel. Father said if we could have the use of it they could put it in the cabin. So it was put in. Now I had taken some quarters of lessons on a piano, and so of course I felt perfectly competent to play most anything. So on this day father and I had a sing and I went on deck a number of times and felt as if I would like sea life ever so much when I became accustomed to the motions of the vessel. The weather was fine and I commenced to feel quite like myself.

February second was another fine day and two vessels in sight. We entered the Gulf Stream. Here again I learned the advantage of experience over mere reading. I had studied about the Gulf Stream at school, but now I was in it and father told me in a few minutes more than a book had in weeks of study. A difference was noticed in the atmosphere. It was several degrees warmer, also the color of the water had changed, it look softer and paler. Gulf weed was seen in large quantities, and "frizzlets," as father called them, pretty enough to put in the neck of my wardrobe. The wake of the vessel was another source of attraction after dark, when a long golden line would extend from the stern of the vessel, all stars and fine sizzlings and boilings.

February fourth was a cloudy day and rough sea and much wind. It was Sunday, father asked the sailors to come into prayers. Four came in and father read and prayed and we all had a sing. One thing father told the sailors was: That he had been to sea with captains who did not acknowledge the Sabbath after three leagues of water, but he should acknowledge it and wished them to. He wanted no unnecessary work, no washing or mending, if they did he should set them to work for him. He also said there was to be no swearing on board the vessel. When they heard him swear then it was time for them to commence. I will say here that during the eighteen months we were gone I heard only three oaths and we brought back to the States four of our original crew.

February fifth, a week today since we left port, and we are in Latitude 34 degrees, 50 minutes N. Longitude 56 degrees, 20 minutes W.

I have fully gotten over the seasickness and am feeling finely. I read and go on deck, watch the ever-changing sea and sky and the men at work. It is most interesting to see how the meals are prepared and what we have to eat.

'One would hardly believe one could have such nice things to eat . . .'

Chapter Four
MEALS AT SEA

O ur meals were brought from the galley, which was down on the main deck, and many a time have I seen a wave catch the steward unawares and soak the dinner so he would have to return for a new supply.

Plenty of good white bread, brown bread, graham bread. Also doughnuts, nice ones without eggs, and once I said to the steward:

"Are you going to the galley?"

"Yes," rising inflection.

"Bring me a doughnut and I will be your grandmother," and with that look that can only come into the face of a Chinaman, he answered:

"How's that?" and for weeks the celestial was in a study over our possible relationship.

Apple dumplings was one of the dishes I used to enjoy and glad to see come onto the table, steamed and a nice sauce, "good enough for poor folks."

How I have regretted my inability to cook. I had never been taught to make a single thing.

Once I remember when mother went away I tried some cream of tartar biscuits, and my younger sister, Annie, showed them to a young gentleman who called, and I felt obliged to put her down cellar. Like a cousin I could "make an apple pie all the crust." We had canned meats of all possible description, fish, tongues and sounds,[G] halibut fins, tripe, ham, bacon, butter in cans, chicken deviled and bedeviled, some of it muchly so, cheese, pickles, vegetables of all kinds, fresh while they lasted, then canned, beans, baked and stewed, peas ditto. "Plum Duff,"[G] the sailor's pride, cracker hash, pilot bread, smoked fish.

At eleven o'clock father and I would have a lunch of split pilot bread, toasted on the stove, raw smoked herring and cheese, before we would go on deck to take the sun to determine our latitude. Flying fish, dolphin, porpoise, turtle all helped to make up a menu.

The medicine chest contained liquor of all kinds and plenty of lime juice.

Day after day we were glad to eat salt meat and bread and still be able to hold on to the seat while we were eating.

Our meals were regular, the cooking good, and the steward always left a lunch in the storeroom at night and many a midnight meal have I eaten.

The second mate eats in the cabin after the captain

has finished and the steward eats then, if he chooses to. I supposed the sailors had the same as the cabin, but I learned they had no table set for them, each one supplies his own tin plate, mug, knife, fork and spoon. They receive their food in large tin pans, great loaves of bread, all they could eat, salt meat one day, salt pork the next, bean soups, pea soup, tea, coffee, molasses and brown sugar twice a week, and on special occasions plum duff.

Water is carried in a large tank, also in casks called "harness casks" and sometimes an allowance is given to every sailor, also there is a food allowance to each sailor, but our sailors were never put on food allowance and only once on water allowance.

The cook washes dishes in a large tank hung on the back of the stove, and when we arrived in Australia only one teaspoon remained for the cabin use, he had missed them in the deep tank and they had been thrown overboard.

In port, everything was furnished that funds could supply, but if I could go to sea again, how many good dishes I could prepare!

Quite a number of flying fish flew on board and were fried, porpoise steak, that tasted like pigs liver, a dolphin was caught and eaten up clean. So you see, although months from port no one need to go hungry unless the unexpected should happen, and then it must be a terrible thing.

'My first sight of albatross,
also whale birds
and sword fish.'

Chapter Five

AT SEA

S econd week at sea and I find the time passing very fast. The ship is in latitude 27 degrees, 30 minutes N. and longitude 39 degrees, 42 minutes W. The mate who has been quite sick, and threatened with a fever, is much better. Father stands watch for him. My first whale is seen this week and a lot of gulf weed was brought on board in which I found some crabs and thought I would save them so I pinned them up on the wall over the bath tub to dry. One day while father was taking a bath I heard him groan, and I asked him what was the matter.

"Those old crabs have fallen down into the water and I thought they were spiders."

Speaking of spiders. I don't wonder he groaned, for later I saw spiders in the cabin so large I was afraid to go to sleep, and that is an actual fact. Their bodies would measure one and one-half inches across, to say nothing of the length of their legs. I remember I shut my stateroom door one night for fear they would get me.

Black fish were seen this week.

Candy making, reading, music on deck, and study, helps to pass the time away. I liked the study of navigation very much. Father promised me a black silk dress if I would answer sixty-seven questions in navigation and sailing, a captain has to answer to get a steamship, and I did answer all questions, and he gave me fifty dollars to buy my dress.

The moonlight evenings are beautiful to behold and I enjoy them very much indeed. I watch the sailors tack ship, so there is always something new coming to interest me.

Mr. Whitmore and myself have taken up the study of Spanish and take turns in reciting to each other. Generally the lessons are studied on top of the sugar locker in the stateroom. I learned to find the latitude by the Polar Star and also to find variation of the compass, and commence to feel that I am getting to be quite a navigator already.

We are making slow progress for this time of year and I keep adding new knowledge in navigation.

Flying fish for breakfast, they fly on board. It is quite a sight to see a school go by the vessel. They are very good eating.

On the twenty-third of February we passed a homeward bound ship and raised the American flag and signal that spells the vessel's name, R. S. P. V., which in the code of signals spells *Charles Stewart*. We also sent up the signal: "Report me all well." We are in hopes to be reported and the home folks see it and know where we are. I have seen mother take up the Boston "Semi-Weekly Journal"[G] many a time and looked at "Spoken," but I never realized before how much it meant to her.

Still good weather and plenty to do and to see. We pass St. Paul de Lo[a]ondo, four tall pyramids of stone arising out of the Atlantic off the coast of Brazil.

March first. We cross the line.[G] The sailors asked father if they could duck me when we crossed the line, "Why she has crossed the line four times," said father. So their fun was spoiled. We are in the doldrums at the equator and many vessels in sight. Our first porpoise was caught this week by a sailor who harpooned it from the forward chains. From its stomach was taken fishes eye balls and some shells that look like bills from birds or turtles. I still have them with me. Two sharks were caught this week, father harpooning one and Mr. Whitmore the other. I discovered them following the vessel and asked the man at wheel what they were when he said sharks I was all excitement and went and called father. The second mate oiled his boots with porpoise oil and nearly drove us out of the cabin. I had always been taught that it was boiling hot at the equator, but it has not been so in this experience. There have been a great many sails in sight this week.

Fifth week. A quiet week at sea. A few vessels and one man-of-war seen. The usual amount of fishes, birds, music and study, and Mr. Whitmore loosing two hats overboard, help to pass the hours away.

A large steamer passed us quite close this week and afterwards a large fly came into the cabin and I am sure it must have come from that steamer, for we have not had a fly since we left port. The steamer passed us in the night and was a pretty sight.

The sixth week at sea finds us off Rio Janerio. Nothing of special importance has happened. We have had a heavy squall that lashed the water into mountains. One vessel seen, and if I could only describe to you what the wind can do. This vessel was about two miles away, which at sea is very near, at times she was in plain view and then no vessel to be seen, and she would reappear and looked so weird coming out of the water. She was the last vessel we saw until we reached Australia.

Week the seventh has been a week of ocean life. My first sight of albatross, also whale birds and sword fish. I have been feeding the albatross on slush and fishing for them with hook and line, and brought three on board and they were sea sick and paid the usual tribute to Neptune. I work hard on navigation. Moonlight evenings keep me on deck. Moving along in a quiet way towards the Cape of Good Hope. So many whale birds around, they are very queer, are grey in color and have very long pointed tails and when a strong wind is blowing they look as if they would turn over backwards.

Eighth week commences with the prospect of land, Gough's Island,[G] latitude 40 degrees, 48 minutes S.; longitude 12 degrees, 4 minutes W. Father asked me to reckon up and see what time we ought to sight land. I did so, and made it about midnight. He shaped a course at four P.M. and I was to be called if land appeared. At twelve o'clock midnight a cry of "Land ho!" brought me out of my bunk and I went on deck to see in the midnight gloom a mountain right ahead, which went to prove how correctly our chronometers had kept their time and how apparently a simple matter it is—after you know how—to find yourself on the globe's surface in the midst of a vast ocean.

We caught an albatross this week that measured twelve feet from tip to tip of wing. Cold weather, mighty seas. I have on mittens when I go on deck. Such mountains of water. Oh! how does the water get into such size and thrash and roll around?

I thought the vessel had struck a rock, but it proved to be a barrel of hard bread that had broken loose from its moorings and was rolling about the cabin. I find that I was commencing to put on avoirdupois; how I discovered it I do not know but that is what is recorded in the diary.

Monday, April 2, 1883. This has been a terrible day, and experience. A gale yesterday made the seas mountain high, and the vessel was kept under more sail had been added. I was standing in the forward gangway door, while father and the mate were watching for a glimpse of the sun. An immense sea came on board from the stern and port quarter, over the house it came in torrents and lifted the mate off of his feet, nearly taking him overboard, but for father reaching out and grasping him, he would have gone. The water came into the gangway and wet my feet. I rushed down stairs, when lo and behold, the cabin was all awash and father's stateroom windows broken in. I returned to tell father, who followed me down and at that moment the mate discovered that the wheel had been carried away and the man missing. He called all hands aft and father rushed out and tackles were called for to keep the rudder in place to keep the ship from broaching to! My thoughts were for the man and I went to look out aft and found him up against the house, the blood running down his face, and a groan coming from his lips. After the safety of the vessel was secured they brought Tom[G] into the cabin and placed him on a lounge and found that his leg was broken between the knee and ankle of the right leg. The steward and two sailors came down and took up the water that was rolling around while father, the mate and myself set the man's leg. Rubber boots had to be removed, and with my scissors I cut up pants, overalls and underdraws and two pairs of stockings. The leg had broken so as to push the bone through the skin, a compound fracture. It took two hours to secure his leg and he was brave. Barrel staves were made into splints and with hole bored in the ends were secured with tape. At one time the mate was nearly overcome. I think it the only time I ever saw him white. Red was the natural color of his face, also the color of his hair.

The man was carried to the second mate's room and later on to the forecastle where he could be with the men. Twice did he undo his leg so that finally father had a long narrow box made to fit his leg, and placing the leg in it packed it with sand and so we took him to Hobart.

The wound was stubborn in healing, but by careful attention my father succeeded in conquering.

When we arrived at Hobart he was at once removed to the hospital where he must remain for three months.

The doctors made a careful examination and congratulated father upon his skill and success while out to sea. We left poor Tom with three months pay in advance and plenty of tobacco. We never heard of him afterward.

Later on the steward said to father:

"Cappy, your daughter dammee smart girllie, smart like hellee. She no go bed and cye. She bailee water like hellee."

Fair winds are sending us towards our destination. Thought much of my sister Annie this week who passed her fourteenth birthday.

While standing in the storm house[G] window an

immense whale spouted so near the vessel I screamed and brought father on deck, he thought a man was overboard. We are off the Cape of Good Hope, but too far south to meet any vessels.

The tenth week starts in with bean soup, canned fresh beef, potatoes, turnips and mince pie for dinner. How is that for a menu in mid-ocean, and ten weeks from port?

Fair winds and sunny skies, high seas and wet deck make up the week with a glass of hot composition at night furnished by the mate.

A hurricane of terrific force marks our eleventh week at sea. Standing at the storm house window, mountain of sea abeam and ahead, looks as if they would deluge us. It is still a wonderful mystery how a vessel can live in such raging seas; all I could do was to sit in father's birth and brace myself for a moments comfort, and still I would not have missed this experience for any amount.

April 26, 1883. Latitude 44 degrees, 13 minutes S. Longitude 100 degrees, 23 minutes E. I pass my eighteenth birthday. Father gave me a five dollar gold piece. Alas! I cannot spend it here. Fifteen years ago I was on the Pacific Ocean. This finds me in the Indian Ocean anxious to see Tasmania Land. Snow storm and snow balling one of the recreations of the week.

On May 3 was awakened by father at ten A. M., as a fearful storm was blowing. The vessel "hove to"[G] for twelve hours. Away overhead a mountain of water, in an instant we are suspended in air on the crest of that mountain, and still we live. This has been a long, hard sail and I find I am longing for land to get a rest from this endless tossing. Father says it is one of the roughest voyages he ever made.

Fourteen weeks at sea on May 7th, and shall now commence to look for land. On May 10th sighted the shores of Tasmania. One hundred and one days from New York.

We sail along to Tasman[G] river, making South Brundy [Bruny] Light[G] at six P. M., pass Tasman Head[G] at six thirty P. M., made Iron Pot Light[G] at eight thirty P. M., here is where we burned a blue flash light over the stern for a pilot, but none came out to us and we continued to sail up the river. The shores were plainly outlined against the sky.

Father and the mate on the top gallant forecastle[G] watching the shores and bends of the river. The second mate midships sending orders along to the man at the wheel. I watch the chart for rocks and shoals that may be in the way. So we move on. I am fascinated and excitement runs high. At last the many lights of a city loom up ahead of us. Father sailed her pretty well up into the harbor. As the starboard anchor was dropped it fouled and for fear of getting too near the wharf the port anchor was ordered out, so both anchors were run out. This was at eleven forty-five P. M.

Not a boat came out to meet us. Although the sailors weighed anchors to drop us astern and "chantied" while doing so. Still we were let alone. Father said he did not want to run the jib boom through the harbor master's window. Folks on shore who heard the "chantying" thought "it was folks on shore going home late." I could not go to bed until all sail was furled, and in the morning when the harbor master, Capt. Riddal, awoke and looked out, the first object that met his eye was a natty bark, all polished and shining, with the stars and stripes waving to the breeze.

As he came down to his boat to board the vessel the sailors were weighing anchor, while I was at the wheel, dropping the vessel astern. On board he came, a strong burly Englishman.

"Where is your pilot?"

"We did not have one, burned a light but no one answered."

"What kind of a bloody vessel is this to come up into a strange port at night without a pilot and with a woman at the wheel?"

*'No other flag
is so welcomed. . .
as the stars and stripes.'*

Chapter Six

HOBART, TASMANIA

*I*t is astonishing how an American vessel in a foreign
port will attract attention. No other flag is so welcomed
and feted as the stars and stripes.

I awoke on the beautiful day of May 11, 1883, hearing
the sound of voices, and I hasten on deck.

What a sight met my eyes!

A beautiful city! The country rising gradually from
the river to the summit of Mt. Wellington. The City of
Hobart,[G] Tasmania, rests at the base of the rise, clean and
attractive.

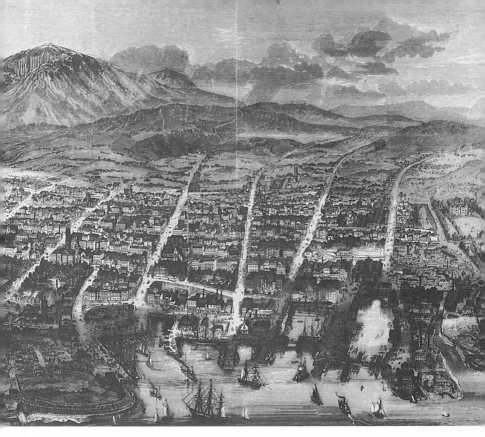

Hobart and Mount Wellington, Tasmania. (Author's Collection)

The harbor master and four assistants came on board, accompanied by the health officer. Quarentine is removed and father goes ashore to the Custom House to enter his vessel; after which he went to the hospital and arranged for the removal of the sailor. Thomas Haney, who had the broken leg, and a carriage arrived at once for him. Next dinner of fresh beef and vegetables was ordered and sent on board, both for the cabin and forecastle.

Well I remember that roast of beef. It was the first roast I had ever seen rolled up. A boat man came with fruit and shells. A dear little girl, five years old, stood on the quay sent by the market man, to bring a welcome, beautiful apples and an invitation to go ashore.

Life friends have they proven. The mother has passed away. The child grown to a beautiful young woman. The nieces married and happy.

A newspaper reporter called for news, which I gladly gave him. He was very pleasant. I scarcely realized I was away from my own country. The day was a busy one. No idle moments, for when I was not engaged with callers I was interested with the sights on shore.

On May 12th went ashore to Mr. Callaghan's, the marketman, and his wife went up town with me to do some purchasing.

Here again was a new experience. English money! But I soon got use to pounds, shillings and pence. I staid on shore to tea. Father joined us in the evening and we all went up town. On Saturday evening it was the custom for everybody to walk out, and the sidewalks and streets were crowded. I came on board for the night, tired and excited.

Dinner at Mr. Callaghan's on Sunday, baked chicken, roast mutton, boiled port, vegetables, pudding and pie, raspberry vinegar. That dinner did taste good. In the afternoon we took a long walk about town, to the cemetery, and home around the shore. Geraniums that we cherish every slip of at home, grow like hedges to all the drives about the cemetery, all came on board the vessel and made a call. It seemed odd to walk on shore and made me quite lame.

They have begun to unload the cargo and everything is much alive with clerks and custom house officers.

The people of Hobart are plain looking, few handsome ones, but their plainness is only skin deep, for they were handsome in acts and friendship.

Home letters arrive and all are well there, while I am here in Australia surrounded with beautiful flowers, and delicious fruit enough to supply a regiment. A friend, Maggie Cusick, takes tea with us, and in the evening, accompanied by Mr. Whitmore, we attend church and meet a number of musical people. The diary says: Met some real nice gentlemen. Ten of them promising to come next Monday evening on board the bark for a sing.

Mr. Whitmore and I take tea with a Mr. Greggits. Here I ate the bread I had heard about, where they spread it before sending it to the table, and have more butter left when they get through than they had when they commenced. Bread cut very thin and the butter actually rubbed into it.

I enjoyed the evening greatly, here was where the American phrases pleased and you could tell by their smiles and glances to each other, when we said something that sounded queer to them, never the less, we also kicked each other under the table once in a while at what we heard. On our return to the bark we found father quite sick and I staid home (onboard) with him until he was all right.

May nineteenth was a gala day. Capt. Riddel, the harbormaster, called and said his daughter would call in the afternoon and take me to a football match. After dinner three jolly Miss Riddels called and we proceeded to the grounds to see the football match between the Cricketers and City teams, the former winning the game. Three young men were added to the list of my acquaintances.

Mr. Wilson, social and cross-eyed.

Mr. Sheriffs, big and might.

Mr. Walch, just right. This of course is very descriptive.

With Maggie I go to my first Roman Catholic church service which I enjoyed very much, the priest preaching a fine sermon from Eccl. 12, 13. On my way home Mrs.

Callaghan loaded me down with good things to eat. Mr. Walch and Mr. Sherrifs call, the former asking me to a concert Monday eve, but I had to decline as I had an engagement. Here again the diary says: "I like Mr. Walch very much, he appears very nicely and is real good looking."

We are unloading very fast and I am sorry, I am having too good a time to want to get away. I buy a treat of cake and candy for my musical friends, who are to come this evening, and have coffee ready when the time comes.

When night came there were twenty-three in the party and I had to send Mr. Florins, the second mate up town for more cake and candy. I thought he would never come back. When he did come I found he had no trouble in getting the cake but the candy was a sticker. He had to go behind the counter and show them what he wanted.

They said: "Oh, lolly pops."

We had a pleasant evening, Maggie helping me do the honors.

We take much enjoyment visiting the different friends. Sometimes it is father and I, sometimes Mr. Whitmore and I. An evening at Capt. Riddel's is always enjoyable. Queen Victoria's birthday on May twenty-fourth, and of course we had to celebrate. At twelve o'clock noon we went to a review of the troops by the Governor, the red coat of the English soldier is very brilliant. Went quite near the Governor, just an ordinary man, stood quite near the cannons when the salute was fired, nearly jumped out of my skin.

After the review we went to the Botanical Gardens.[G] You must always go to these gardens where ever you are, but they are all alike. We met two young men, Mr. Mitchell and Mr. Herburg. It was against the rules to touch a seed, flower or slip, but Miss Riddel, on the sly, would take what she wanted, and drop it into her umbrella. There were some beautiful white lillies called Trumpeter lillies she wanted but did not dare to touch—all she talked about was those lillies. We returned to the bark and had not been there a great while when a knock came at the after gangway door. I went to the door and found Mr. Mitchell with a most beautiful bunch of trumpeter lillies, which he presented to me. I invited him in and when he saw Miss Riddel his face was as good as a poor play; of course I was delighted to get the lillies instead of Miss Riddel.

The girls asked him to favor us with a song and he was willing, the song running something like this:

"There she goes on her little toes, her little tootseys wootsies."

I was ashamed of myself. I had all I could do to keep my face straight, and I am not sure even now that I succeeded. After he had gone we teased Miss Riddel about the lillies, but she took it all good naturedly. Later on Mr. Sheriff and Mr. Wilson called, the latter I believe I stated was cross-eyed. He had a very forceable way of shaking hands. He would grasp the fingers tight, give on tremendous jerk and nearly dislocated your shoulder, by the time you had come back to earth and found you still had a right arm it would be time for him to go and you had to again go through the terrible operation. On my return home I used to entertain my sisters with cross-eyed hand shakes.

The museum I found very entertaining there being many odd things to see peculiar to Tasmania,

On returning home from a turn about town I found the Riddel girls had called and left a basket of tomatoes. I filled the basket with hardbread and Mr. Whitmore and I returned it, and spent a pleasant evening while Miss Isabelle entertains us mimicing different people.

One Sunday afternoon father came into the cabin and said:

"That sick dude is out on the wharf and don't you ask him to stay to supper."

Of course I had no idea who it was, but went out and found Mr. Sheriffs and Mr. Walch, the latter immaculate. He carried a beautiful bouquet of roses. Twenty-three years later; if you should go to the bottom of my trunk in a certain box, you will find a bunch of dried rose buds. They came from Hobart, Tasmania.

I invited them to tea, also Maggie, who had called.

'I see banana trees and sugar cane growing.'

Chapter Seven

LEAVING HOBART FOR BRISBANE

May 30th. Memorial Day at home, but we sail for Brisbane.[G]

I got up a four thirty A. M. and "took the wheel" out of the river, while the men were busy snugging things away for sea.

We are permitted to leave without a pilot as we came up without one, but the Board of Investigation made quite a turnabout it, and pulled the pilots up for not being on the watch. It was a pretty sail down the river by daylight, and I enjoyed it very much.

Mr. Whitmore made a drawing of Iron Pot Light that was very good, and so the day goes on. We sail out of the bay and enter the Pacific Ocean, and in the morning are out of sight of land.

Reaction sets in, I am dull and dumpish all but appetite which is sharkish.

I go to work trying to do up sewing and mending that has been sadly neglected since we were to sea before. Rough seas and pleasant weather, and I contrive to sew when I am not holding on to keep my seat. There has been nothing exciting on our voyage up the coast. We are out of sight of land and see very few vessels or steamers.

On Sunday, June 9th, I woke and came on deck at four thirty A.M. to see land in sight, and staid on deck all day. Many steamers pass us, presumably from Brisbane, and at night see Cape Moreton Light.[G]

We shorten sail so as to wait for daylight to make the bay. I pack up the organ as it was consigned to a Brisbane firm.

June 10th, I was called early by father this morning to find we were right off shore under Cape Moreton Light, and we asked at the signal station for a pilot, but there was none to be had.

We asked if we could anchor and was told "yes," and we signaled to be reported.

It is fascinating, these new scenes. I have been on deck all day long and watched people and teams on shore.

A pilot arrives before daylight and we are glad. We weigh anchor and start for Brisbane. Head winds cause us to tack ship every few minutes for the water is very shallow, and it is a very easy matter to tell where the channel is there is such a difference in the color of the water. We are all day beating up to where we take a tug up the river.[G] We have to anchor for the night, and put the pilot to bed, and on June 12th, at noon, a tug boat comes and takes us in tow and up the narrowest, crookedest river you can imagine, thus we proceed to the city. I look across the country and see a large city.

"What is that," I asked the pilot?

"Brisbane."

And sure enough after turning almost completely around I would not dare to say how many times, we arrive in port.

I see banana trees and sugar cane growing. I thought one field had been mowed and the hay cocked up, but they were great ant heaps. It is three P.M. when we reach Brisbane and father goes ashore to enter his vessel. On return he brings letters from home.

All are well.

It is a pretty place. The city is quite large and built on hills, so it is very showy, while on the other bank is a quiet country village.

In the evening father and I take a walk up town. He said I could have anything I wanted and I chose a pine apple. When we arrived on board I found a gentleman and three young ladies. Their names were Wood, and they were ready to take us body and soul during our stay in port.

'... oh, my! oh, me! ..
I had gotten into
the prickly pears.'

Chapter Eight

BRISBANE

I went to work at once and put down the cabin carpet
and polished up in fine style. The Misses Wood came
down and took me up town shopping. On our return we
had dinner and then I went up to their home, up on a high
hill, but very pretty, where I had passion fruit and colonial
wine, nice also. I came down on board to tea, and father, Mr.
Whitmore and myself started out to go to church, but we
could not find one, so we looked the city over somewhat
and returned home.

I have decided I must have a new hat, so the Wood

Queen Street, Brisbane, 1883. (Courtesy of the John Oxley Library)

girls came down and I was going to take my "black chip of the previous summer" up town, to have it repressed and trimmed. Under the lounges of the cabin were lockers where I kept reading matter and wrapping paper, but the Custom House officer had sealed up all the tobacco in one where wrapping paper was kept. I rushed across the cabin, lifted the cushion, and before I thought lifted the lid and broke the Government seal.

Consternation! I at once went on deck and told father who called an officer. They came down in the cabin and examined my work. The official said:

"It was not properley sealed and I will let it go this time but if it happens again it will be a fine of ten sovereigns."

From shopping we went up to Capt. Woods' where I found father and a young man, I do not remember his name. We staid to tea and in the evening two sea captains called. We played musical chairs and had a lively time. I find the English people very fond of games.

I had just finished up my four household duties when father came in followed by a gentleman and lady. Father was carrying a very cunning baby. They were Mr. and Mrs.

Webster, Swedish consul and wife. After a pleasant call we accepted an invitation to dinner on Sunday.

When the day arrived we crossed the river and were warmly welcomed. Father was invited into a room without the ladies for an appetiser. Of course I was curious to know what was going on. Later I learned that salt fish, gin and crackers were served. I did not see any reason for barring out the ladies.

At dinner we had soup, roast mutton, baked chicken, vegetables, three kinds of pickles, bread and German beer. For dessert, plum pudding, Swedish pudding, oranges, apples, plums, pears, bananas, dates and colonial wine.

One evening we went shopping and the mate bought his wife a pretty ring, Australian gold with rubies and chip diamonds. The next morning I was ready to receive callers, and heard some one come into the cabin. I looked up to see a fine looking man in uniform.

He said, "How do you do," and made himself at home, took up the photograph album and talked about the pictures and then walked into father's stateroom and sat down at his desk. Then I knew he was either drunk or crazy, and went out and called father, who came in and ordered him out, and when father tried to put him out he resisted, tearing father's coat. Father had him arrested and it was found that he was chief officer on a coast steamer, and was out of jail on bail to make a trip. He begged father not to push the case, and being willing to settle all damages he did so, and I received the money for mending the coat.

I spend a day at Capt. Woods.' I was sitting at the piano and thought I heard some one in the room, but could not see any one; heard the sound again and looked down side me and thought a man's slipper was walking along, but it was a cockroach.

We are unloaded and moored out in the river. The city is very pretty from here. Such numbers of steamers come and go. The coast trade is very large.

Father is busy looking up a freight, while I go on board a large English steamer to lunch. She had just arrived from England with two hundred work girls. I enjoyed the hour I was on board. Such finishings and china and glass. The dainty lunch was served of cold chicken, bread and wine.

Capt. Nordfelt of the bark *Karmen* invited us to lunch, "shnapp" prevailing, while later on all visit me and have Yankee food.

Mr. Whitmore and I visit the Public Garden and meet a number of Aborigines, black and wicked looking, the women have their babies strapped on their backs. Another queer looking people are the Lascars of India. One sees a great many on the steamers.

We are invited on board the *Karmen* to tea. All the Netzler family were there and the Misses Wood. The costumes of the Wood girls beggared description. A black cloth skirt, long black polanaise with garnet sashes certainly a foot wide pinned on with common pins. On one girl we counted twenty pins in sight. Miss Kate Wood staid all night. She returned home in the morning and I counted six old maid pins on the floor. Father was quite pale and asked him what was the matter.

"I was afraid her clothes would drop off before she got home," said father.

At ten o'clock, Capt. Nordfelt, Mr. and Mrs. Netzler and three children, the brother, governess, myself and four sailors from the *Karman* started on a picnic up Brisbane river. We were rowed seven miles and such a jolly time as we did have; went on shore at a pretty spot, built a fire in an old stump and made coffee. A game of tag was played. I ran into some bushes and oh, my! oh, me! when I got out what a condition I was in. I had gotten into the prickly pears and my skirts and stockings were completely lined with prickers. I nearly went crazy. I had to go away by myself and pick those pests out before I could have one moment of comfort. Nevertheless, a prickly pear is very fine eating. We carried three kinds of meat, bread, cake, oranges, bananas, hard bread, pale ale, brandy, gin, wine and two pails of water and coffee, not a crumb or drop was brought back.

It seemed a strange place, not any of the foliage being like any I had seen before.

We arrived back at seven thirty P.M. and had lunch on the *Charles Stewart.*

Ballast is all on board and we expect to sail tomorrow for Valparaiso, Chile. Now commences another series of good bys. I went ashore on the Brisbane side in the forenoon and called on all the good friends, and the Wood girls came on board to dinner for the last time. After they had gone Mr. Whitmore and I went to say good bye to the Netzler family.

Then I came on board finished up some home letters and accounts for father, when he came on board and said we were not to sail until the fourth.

The Glorious Fourth! All flags and bunting set and all the steamers and vessels are bedecked in bunting in honor of the American vessel who is celebrating.

At eight A.M. we weigh anchor and in company with a tug we start down Brisbane river amid the waving of handkerchiefs, dipping of flags, ringing of bells and firing of

Indian crackers. We come to a turn in the river and Brisbane and pleasant friends are left behind forever, but I have had a delightful time. At four P. M. we are anchored in the Moreton Bay[G] to await a fair wind.

How still it is, where have we arrived? After all of the din of the city it seems strange enough. We get out the lines and catch one fish. And night comes on.

'Whales are all about the ship. Light winds, smooth sea.'

Chapter Nine
ONCE MORE AT SEA

Thursday, July 5, 1883, we once more put out to sea. Find a rough sea and everybody pretty well shaken up, but onward we go hoping to make Valparaiso, Chile, in thirty-five days.

How rough the seas are. I have been sick for days, not being able to sit up, eat or sleep. Father thinks I got tired out, and that the warm days and cold nights had a good deal to do with it.

On July 12th we are off the Island of New Zealand and I am much improved, but we are making slow progress. On the fifteenth I go on deck for the first time since we left port. Whales are all about the ship. Light winds, smooth sea.

On July 17th we cross the 180 degree of longitude, finding ourselves in west longitude, and so we gain a day.

We shall have two Tuesdays this week. At first it seemed strange, but as father talked it over I could see how it all came about.

There is nothing specially exciting; winds moderate. Father bought me an accordian in Brisbane but I can not learn to play it. The nights are beautiful. Cape pigeons, whale birds and albatross are plenty. Good breezes are blowing us across the Pacific Ocean but the trip will be long. I am writing letters home so as to have them ready when I get into port to send at once.

It grows colder as the trip lengthens and we have a fire in the cabin and find it very pleasant. I am studying Spanish faithfully, for that is the Chilians' language.

Rough seas, short sails, pleasant skies and on we go to our destination.

We are twenty-six weeks from New York; weather cold and blustering, headwinds, and going too far to the south, but what can we do?

Father and I pass the time away with navigation, lunches of herring and hardbread, talking of the folks at home and our many Australian friends.

The mate catches a "poly-poll," in other words a bird.

On August 1st we have clam chowder for dinner and the vessel heading S. E. by E. 1-2 E. This is entertaining. I keep pegging away at navigation and Spanish, and each day I pick off the day's work on the chart. Have learned this week to reckon latitude by the meredian, at last we have found a fair wind and are sailing our course.

This twenty-eighth week is one continuous roll. The worst I have ever experienced. It seems as if the vessel will tip over. I can only read and study. Reading a book entitled *The Ministry of Life*,[G] it seems to impress me that it is perfectly wonderful that some people can be so good at all times and in all places. Strange also that it is always in printer's ink that we meet them, but never in the flesh.

The last of the week is calmer and pleasant. I learn to reckon latitude by the Moon.

Cape pigeons and one old albatross about, and I find the new week beginning with sailors in to prayers; fair weather and good progress.

I have started on my twenty-ninth week with slush bucket, tempting the birds, and have succeeded in catching some cape pigeons, but they were so seasick I was glad to put them overboard.

I am passing the time away with necessary work, and reading *Oliver Twist*.

We are anticipating land at no great distance.

Father discovers a ship off of the weather bow.

The mate is "catting"[G] the anchors ready for port.

On Wednesday, Aug. 22, in the forenoon, father discovers land off the weather bow.

The Andes, in the distance, land about fourteen miles away and a fair wind. After taking the wheel for the men to wear[G] ship, I stayed on deck and watched the volcanos of the Andes. As darkness comes on I count thirteen volcanic fires on the tops of the mountains and it is a great sight. I had no idea I should ever see such sights, and after arising early on Aug. 23rd and watching the shores grow nearer each hour, we anchor to a buoy at two thirty P. M., with six arrivals and many ships in port. Business men flock on board and it seems real good to see new faces.

'The aunt was very pleasant...
and sent a basket
of delicious fruit...'

Chapter Ten

VALPARAISO

Valparaiso is a cozy looking place at the foot of a steep mountain. After all was quiet and father had returned from entering his vessel, I finished up home letters and went to bed, to awake at daybreak and go on shore to meet friends, who years ago welcomed father, mother and myself, a child of three years of age, to Valparaiso.

Mr. John Bates, who remembered father well—and who would not that had seen him once—made us at home in his office, and his daughter, Miss Bates, was very kind to

Valparaiso. (The Kendall Whaling Museum, Sharon, MA.)

me, and took me about the city and to the Public Gardens and to her aunt's, and such style! I can feel the touch of that velvet carpet now. I thought I had stepped on the cat but she was silent, and the next step set me right, and I realized on what I was walking. Those gold chairs looked rather shaky, but I sat down after a fashion. I remember perfectly how I felt. I believe that salon was half a mile across, at least that was the impression it gave me. The aunt was very pleasant and served cake and wine and sent a basket of delicious fruit down to the vessel.

Father's day to celebrate I think, for he had a tooth pulled and a hair cut, probably he needed the hair cut for I had been his barber on board the vessel, as well as the

mate's, so I guess a little trimming up would not hurt either of them. Father used to say that I was the only barber that sat down on his back while cutting his hair.

I was in the barber shop waiting for father and there were four other men having their hair cut. An attendant had swept the hair up all behind father's chair. When he looked round and saw the pile of hair—being himself extremely bald headed—he pretended they had cut all the hair off his head. He pointed to the pile of hair on the floor and then would rub his head, at last they saw the joke and all had a good laugh.

Valparaiso looks as if some one had picked it up and then dropped it down in a bunch. I staid on shore until six

P. M. and when we went on [b]oard, a two and a half mile row, I got my red, black, green and yellow plaid dress soaked, but it stood the test well.

One day we took a walk and the first thing we knew we were face up to a mountain, the street ended because it could go no farther.

Mr. Ben Bates takes us about the city and later we go on [b]oard the bark *Olive Thurlow*[V] of New York, Capt. Corbett, who has his wife and three children with him.

I spend a day on board the bark *Innerwick*[V] of Nova Scotia, Capt. Waters, who has his wife and a friend, Miss Bayne, with him. We had a nice dinner and tea and a ride about the city in the horse cars, that have a top story on them.

Father sent the ship's stores on board. Many nice things among them being nuts, loaf sugar and honey. Possibly I can not eat this last commodity.

When I was nine years old my mother let me visit an uncle who kept a great many bees, and for the time I had all the honey I wanted.

Some time after I got home, mother bought a lot of honey and had it in the storeroom, and I used to go in on the sly and eat and eat. Finally I got enough and when we came to have some for supper I could not eat any. Mother was quite surprised, knowing how fond I was of the article, and said:

"What is the matter Hattie that you do not want any?"

"Oh, I got cloyed of it when I was in Kenduskeag."

As my sisters knew what was the real trouble, one only had to mention honey and someone would say: "I don't wish for any I got cloyed when I was in Kenduskeag." On Thursday I was on shore all day with father, and when I got tired I went into Mr. Bates' office to rest. The clerks were all very kind and offered me cigarettes, and were quite surprised to find I did not smoke, as they thought all American ladies smoked, but all the smoking I had ever indulged in up to that time was when a chum cousin of mine and I used to smoke clay pipes and sweet fern in Old Deacon Herrick's pasture, and play we were Indians.

We went to dinner at an English hotel and here was where we met so many sea captains. Father has chartered the vessel to go to the Lobos de Afuera Islands, off the coast of Peru to load guano[G] for Gibralter, Spain, for orders.

Capt. Corbett has sailed for there and Captains Waters and Roy are to sail for the same port, so we take our friends with us. We have chicken dinner and all the fixings.

On Friday I go shopping. Mr. Whitmore goes with me to talk Spanish. He does pretty well at the business. I am no good.

I buy all necessary things, no luxury, I don't think at that time I knew enough to buy a pretty thing, for if I did why did not I get them? I would go shopping and buy only what was absolutely needed.

Mr. Whitmore goes on board to prepare for sea and I make my farewell calls, arriving on board at one o'clock P. M. and at quarter past two we leave the buoy headed for the Lobos Islands.

I leave Valparaiso as elsewhere with regrets and pleasant recollections.

The ships *Innerwick* and *Esther Roy*[V] are both sailing with us.

Sept. 1st finds us at sea again and the days go by uneventfully until Sept. 8th when we arrive at the Lobos Islands.

' We all go ashore… and got large booby eggs, dark blue.'

Chapter Eleven
LOBOS DE AFUERAG

As the fog lifts on Sept. 8th at three P. M., we discover the island right ahead and are anxious to arrive before night which we do, dropping anchor just ten minutes after the bark *Innerwick*.

I am up bright and early to look at the island, such a lonesome looking place, bunches of rocks, one lone house, but the seas are magnificent. The southeast trade winds blow in and send the waves sixty feet up the rocks and how they roar as they climb up and boil as they come back.

Birds, birds, birds, and they dive from great height.

A stone as big as your head could not fall any straighter, and up they come with a fish in their mouth.

The sea lions vie with the waves, seeing which can make the most noise, and one small island shines in the sun just from their slimy bodies who crawl upon it, so as to completely cover it. A hammer headed shark was a great curiosity, he came right along side of the vessel, his head looking like a nail keg put on sideways.

I saw a fight between two whales some distance out and they made the water fairly foam with their great tails.

As for mackeral, they tip the water so you would think it was raining great drops, and as far as the eye can reach they can be seen. Rock cod abound, and such handsome fish and fine eating. We salted some to take to sea.

The captain of the port called and was very pleasant and informed us that the governor would call later on. What shall I wear?

I learn that there are more houses around the island, where the governor, captain of the port, doctor and chemist live. There are twenty-six vessels in port.

Monday a steamer is expected and all the captains are going aboard to see if they can buy fruit and fresh meat, but they could not get any. I went on board the *Innerwick* and had a pleasant time.

A bark arrives today. The *Eudora*[V] of Nova Scotia, Capt. Fulton, who has his wife with him. Her weight must surely be three hundred pounds, she was dressed in a light pink wrapper and pulled lines with the sailors. It was a funny sight. Days later it was as good as a circus to see her try to land in a row boat from a vessel's gangway. At one time, in Capt. Casey's boat, we had to come along side ten times, by actual count, before we landed her and then she nearly swamped the boat.

A gang plank like a pair of stairs is let down one side of a vessel and a small platform at the bottom. These immense waves would bring the boat to the platform and one must jump into the boat at once or the wave would carry the boat by, and then it would have to come back again.

There are some pretty crafty natives here who travel in a raft called a "Catamaran," which consists of a few logs tied together. It is a puzzle to me where they got their logs for not a tree grows on the island, not even a blade of grass.

Another American ship has joined the fleet. The ship *John C. Potter,*[v] Capt. Curtis, wife and daughter three years old.

I am the youngest woman in the fleet, and make most of the calls, going in the first boat that calls for me, or by appointment.

We all go ashore on an egg hunt and got large booby eggs, dark blue. Handsome crabs. The coloring of the dead crabs being beautiful. I found many shells that looked like false teeth on a diminuative scale.

Miss Bayne and I thought we would go in wading as the men had all gone to hunt eggs. So we took off our shoes and stockings and went to step into a lovely clear looking place, and as we stepped in a great yellow water snake moved himself away as he feared contamination, I suppose. But I can say right here, we at once changed our minds and gave him the right of way of the water of the Pacific Ocean. He was a nasty looking thing.

We are moored stem and stern,[G] and the only way we can travel is by boat, but everybody's boat is always ready to carry you anywhere you care to go. At five P. M. Mrs. Curtis sent her boat and mate to say that Capts. Curtis and Fulton went fishing in the morning and had not returned,

Loading guano at Chincha Island. (Louis S. Martel Photo, Mystic Seaport)

and she was getting anxious. Would father see if he could find them, and would I come and stay with her?

Of course I went gladly, while father got a number of boats out to look for the missing captains.

They were found an hour later clinging to a rock, every wave washing over their heads, and were so exhausted they were about ready to give up the struggle. While returning home an undertow had capsized the boat and thrown them into the water, and by good luck only were they saved. They were brought home, two sailors being with them, and were soon as well as ever.

We staid on board to tea, and after one of the nicest gin-slings I ever drank, father and I returned home.

Fishing, visiting and calls fill up the time until Sept. 18th when we go on shore to celebrate the Independence of Chili.

We went up to the Governor's where we were received with open arms. Refreshments of fruit jellies, cake and wine were served. A regatta in which our boat, manned by two of our sailors and two of Capt. Curtis' won the race.

A greased pig race was very exciting, but finally the pig ran into a hut and was captured. After a pleasant afternoon, we returned to the *J. C. Potter* where we had tea, and came home.

On the following day the governor and the captain of the port called.

I wish I were an artist and could draw a few figures and features! Nevertheless they were real attractive and had a pleasant call from them. Father told them how he had four daughters, and the fellows swung on the front gate so much, it broke the hinges and he had to take it off.

The governor said:

"I would like to swing on some American girl's front gate" but I did not get a chance to say "yes," but don't I wish you could have seen him?

The little black goatee is fresh in my memory.

The Doctor was really quite nice. His face made me think of a glass of gin fizz. Little downy whiskers that made me think of fizz, little eyes that looked like sparkles, and a complexion that looked like gin.

The mate who spoke the Spanish language somewhat, wanted a tooth pulled; so he told the doctor:

"The last one in the row."

Now there was a good sound grinder way back, but the mate meant on the end of the unbroken row. The doctor grasped the grinder and out it came. The mate just danced a regular jig, and would not let him pull the tantalizer, but finally, after two days he succumbed, and had the tooth pulled.

An English bark finished loading today and went out to sea. While weighing anchor the sailors "chantyed" and it was just fine, their voices were so soft and they sang along so smoothly, I enjoyed it very much.

Our sailors used to "chanty" once in a while, but it was no such music as that.

The melody of the "chanty" songs are just as sweet as they can be. "Ranzo," "I'm bound for the Rio Grande," "Whiskey Jonny," "If ever I live to get on shore," and many others.

The ladies went ashore and met with Mr. and Mrs. McDonald. Mr. McDonald is the agent for the guano company, and we are taken over millions of tons of bird deposit, dead birds and eggs, almost as solid as masonry, and ammonia enough to clear the lungs at any time. Mrs. McDonald served a dainty lunch and orangeade, and then we all came home.

The day following Mrs. McDonald and myself spent the day with Mrs. Curtis, the gentlemen coming to tea and spending the evening.

Capt. and Mrs. Waters gave a large party on the *Innerwick*. All the ladies of the fleet invited, and the gentlemen coming later on.

They were highly entertained by father who used the edge of the dining table for a piano, and sang the following song:

"Said the young Obediah, to the old Obediah, Diah, Obediah, Obediah, Obediah," putting in all the demi-semi-quivers, and most of the folks had a good laugh, but two English ladies "looked like meat axes" and had that expression on their face, of pity for one so far gone as father appeared. It was a performance I had seen since childhood so I was not disturbed.

The days up to October first were divided among the fleet, calling and receiving callers.

Mrs. Curtis and I went on shore to spend the day at Mrs. McDonald's to meet her sister who had just arrived from the mainland. We had a nice visit and lovely fruit brought by the steamer. I was weighed an tipped the scales at one hundred and fifty pounds.

Vessels are finishing loading every day now and at night they celebrate with an illumination. It looks very pretty across the water.

The days pass, old faces leave and new faces come.

A vessel arrived the 20th, Bark *Yula*,[v] whose commander, Capt. Hall, was the pleasantest of them all. I wish he had arrived earlier.

We finish loading and I go on board the *Innerwick* to see our illumination. Of course this means sea, and I shall have to say good bye to all these good people.

I made a farewell trip over the island and said goodbye to all the island folks, called on the fleet for the same purpose and on Saturday, October the twenty-seventh, we are towed out to sea by forty row boats. Captain Hall, Waters and Roy going around the island with us. After all the goodbys we said we lost sight of the island at six P.M.

'Penguins every where,
they chase each other
and make me think of frogs.'

Chapter Twelve
AWAY FOR GIBRALTER

At sea again after a sojourn of seven weeks among pleasant friends and ever changing events. Foggy weather, but fair winds send us bounding towards Cape Horn. I busy myself packing away my "dresses" and as I have not had a new one since I left home you can imagine how much exertion it takes. I keep busy knitting a "Tam-o-shanter" for father. How I wish you could see that "Tam" knit by guess from ravelled out stocking legs, perched on the head of a man six feet two inches tall, weighing two hundred and fifty pounds.

A first-class cartoonist would pale with envy.

I keep busy mending and studying. The mate has a blue pea jacket, if I patched the lining of that jacket once I did on an average, every other day, sometimes I used to think he sat up night cutting them out so I would have something to do. If I ever had it to do again I would put them in with copper rivets.

Fleas are a great attraction, or else we are a great attraction for the fleas; almost every night I hear, "Hattie, see if you can't catch this flea."

I light my candles and start in, he is found hidden away in the woolen blanket, executed, and I return to my bunk. This was continued the rest of the voyage, and unless it gets too bad I shall not refer to it again; it recalls too many unhappy moments.

With pleasant weather, pickling onions, watching for ships headed for California, watching the birds and fishes, reading, singing, studying, and albatross fishing, we reach our fortieth week at sea. One large albatross that we caught walked to the galley and ate a pound of salt pork from the steward's hand. Beautiful nights! I spend hours on deck. As we go south the days lengthen and it is light nearly all the twenty-four hours.

Father and I are busy making chetney. I find we cooked for four hours a mixture of the following ingredients: Peaches, onions, raisins, sugar, pepper, salt and vinegar. It is recorded as smelling nice.

Rough weather sets in and the vessel rolls and pitches fiercely, and on November twenty-third we pass a vessel, the first we have seen since we left the islands. I saw my first penguin today, they are chasing the vessel. This shows that we are getting south. They dive from great heights and can be seen swimming under water a great ways. When they come to the surface they make a loud noise. In those days I did not know what to liken it to, but in these days I should call it an "Automobile Honk."

It is now necessary to have a fire in the cabin, the weather is so cold. Winds fair, wet deck, so I do not go out much, and I console myself by making chocolate creams; wish I had known how to make fudge.

Birds! I wonder how many I have seen since I reached the coast of South America, surely millions of them, all sizes and kinds.

Thanksgiving day, and we have canned chicken, corn, mashed potatoes, maccaroni, mince pie and nuts for dinner, not so bad way out in the Pacific Ocean, but I cannot say how it agreed with me, for I note that on the next day we had hot whiskey.

I catch a bird galled a "goamp,"[G] if you know what that is. He was a pretty dark brown on his head, his back light gray, and had white rings around his eyes that gave him a ghostly appearance.

We welcome fair winds, and on December second we make the Island of Diego Ramares.[G] This island is just south of the Horn and seemed uninhabited and thickly covered with evergreen. There are two vessels in sight; one always feels that they have visitors when vessels are in company. Penguins every where, they chase each other and make me think of frogs. I laughed aloud to see them play. We have only had bean soup five times this week. The steward took us at our word; every time beans would appear some one would say: "What, more beans; it does seem nice to see beans," and next meal would appear steward and beans, served with a smile of satisfaction. One day while making candy, a piece of greased paper fell on to the stove and it smelled so like beef steak that it gave rise to a longing for some home cooking.

The seas are simply terrible, one that came on board was about as large a one as father ever saw. There is nothing to do during such weather but to hold on.

On December nineteenth we signal a ship bound to London from Sydney, Australia, forty-five days out, she wished us a pleasant passage, and "had we spoken any vessels?" She was flying the English flag.

Whales and sharks about us, and we have dolphin for dinner. These are the fish that turn seven colors before they die.

We signal another ship, flying a German flag, but did not learn her name. She asked to be reported "all well." This we will gladly do. Now you will ask: How can you report a ship when you do not know her name? We will report the code letters that spell her name, and it is registered so all shipping offices know what vessel is meant.

On Christmas father put a five dollar gold piece in my stocking, a piece of bread, five wooden tooth picks, a box of pepper, an empty shaker bottle and an empty beef jar. For dinner we had fresh canned beef, maccaroni, potatoes, tomatoes, plum duff, nuts and raisins.

The weather being much warmer I put on a thin dress. We had a ship in company, *The Collingwood*,[v] for London. She had a lady and gentleman on board who looked like passengers.

The lady had on a black skirt. red shawl, buff polanaise,[G] black hat and white apron. She was not dressed very stylishly, and it set me to wondering how many older sisters she had.

The last day of the old year finds us speeding towards the equator. Trade winds, sailors painting ship. The day has been beautiful and ends with a beautiful sunset.

*'Now the water is full of
sargossa weed and "frizzelets."
Portugese man-of-war...'*

Chapter Thirteen

ONWARD WE GO

*A*t twelve o'clock last night I was awakened by the worse noise, just outside my window. The man at the wheel struck eight bells, followed by bell ringing, fog horns roaring, men shouting and a most terrible noise made by blowing through a great tunnel.[G] I was frightened at first but father said:

"I wish you a Happy New Year."

We are surely creeping north for the northern constellations are coming into sight, and let me speak here of a beautiful southern constellation. The Southern Cross.[G] It looks suspended about half way between heaven and earth.

Over the line on January tenth and speeding towards port. At half past five in the morning I heard the men talking about a vessel and I got up to see it, and right across our bow sailed a three-masted schooner, with no side lights out, and they saw her just in time to save a collision. Heavy showers; I enjoy them. The water comes down in torrents, and a thunder storm during which the lightening seems to play through the rigging.

The discovery of a comet^G is reported by the second mate and he calls all the cabin dwellers on deck, and sure enough there was a beauty, with a long shiny tail, at the same time we saw also the north star.

January nineteenth, I do up my "crimps"^{G} for the first time since last September. I suppose I wanted to get used to myself so as to know whom to introduce to the crowned heads of Europe. On the same day I dressed up in my black bunting dress. I suppose I thought it best to dress up gradually so as not to become vain when I came to that red, green, yellow and black plaid. Now the water is full of sargossa weed and "frizzelets." Portugese man-of-war—a little animal that looks like a pink bubble on the water. Whales and vessels.

More preparations for royalty.

I took my black beaver hat, cut off some of the brim, bent it into poke shape, put my bright bird across the front and some black satin ribbon across the back; I felt quite proud. I donned the hat and went on deck—for father had been quite anxious over what I was doing—with the full determination that after I had startled Europe, the style was so lasting I would keep if for the show window of Jordan, Marsh & Co.^{G} of Boston, but father ordered the hat overboard, however my humane heart would not allow me to drown the bird, so I removed it to a place of safety, but do not remember the final disposition of the same.

Lost the trade winds on January twenty-sixth. Awoke in the morning to hear the "doldrum birds sing"—that is the booms creaking as they swing with the motion of the vessel. As we were about through dinner on the 27th, the second mate called down the forward gang way:

"A rock or wreck off the port bow."

"How far way," asks the captain.

"About four miles, sir."

I did not want any more dinner. Father asked me to go to the chart and see if any there were any rocks about us, and I found none.

I took the telescope and went on deck to see what looked to be a large rock.

When father came on deck he ordered the course of the vessel changed so as to bring us nearer. As we drew nearer we could plainly see that it was the wreck of a vessel about the size of our own, bottom side up. A grewsome sight! It made me feel both sick and sad. It would rise on a wave with a sort of hiss and a swash, about half its length, and then plunge into the next one with a groan that was almost human.

It was the saddest sight I had seen, and such a danger to navigation! If the wind had not breezed up, father would have sent men in a boat to cut a hole in her and send her to the bottom. Her sides were covered the barnacles and many sharks and fishes could be seen around her. It almost made me sick. The wreck was in latitude 33 degrees and 35 minutes north, longitude 36 degrees. 01 minute W.

A year from New York. Rough weather. I got my ironing all done up and laid it on my bed, my window was open, when in came a sea through my stateroom window and wet my ironing, bed and all. Such is "life on the ocean wave."

It is quite an anticipation to know where we will go from Gibralter, for we have not the least idea, as we are under orders.[G]

Father is not very well. A bad trouble with his eyes, some days he is real miserable and I feel quite anxious about him, and hope he will be better when we get into port.

We are bounding along two hundred miles a day; seven hundred miles from Gibralter. Moderate and variable winds throw the vessel aback, so I take the wheel while the sailors wear[G] ship.

Feb. 7th the excitemant begins. We are up to the Straits of Gibralter, but the wind is dead ahead and we have to stand off from the land, and we are all day backing and filling, because we cannot get through the Straits. Vessels on every hand are doing the same as we are and as anxious.

During the night I went out on deck to see a bark pass us about a mile away, in the moonlight. She had painted ports and looked weird, but so handsome. It seemed like a picture by moonlight.

I am awakened by the mate telling father there was land ahead, and so I am up at once and on deck, and find the Straits right ahead, and in company with us are three vessels, and we can see the smoke of fourteen steamers.

At eight P. M. we are up to Cape Spartel.[G] We slowly creep up through the Straits. I am too excited to sleep, and am on deck all night. At Tarifa[G] a light is seen, also a fort. It is six A. M. We get up opposite the rock at ten A. M. A tug comes out and she offers to take us in, but her price was too much, and at two P. M. another tug takes us into the harbor and under the shadow of the famous Fort of Gibralter, Feb. 11, 1884.

'a sight of monkeys great and small, jabbering and jumping as free as air.'

Chapter Fourteen
GIBRALTER

*T*his is a pretty place. The port is closed in by a mighty wall, and high up on the sides of the rocks are seen the port holes for the great guns that guard the Straits of Gibralter. They have guns that can send shot across to the coast of Africa, twelve miles away.

On the very summit is a signal station.

Father went on shore and entered his vessel, but is obliged to come on board by six P. M. or he will be locked into the city unless he has a permit from the governor. He brings the home letters; one said death, all the rest well.

The rock of Gibraltar. (G. W. Blunt White Library, Mystic Seaport)

The City of St. Roque,[G] at the head of the bay has a very pretty position up on the summit of a hill, and a great many cities and towns on the Mediterranean are built that same peculiar way.

I could not go on shore the 12th, because it was a stormy day, but I made good use of it. A number of callers came on board, and I wrote many letters. At night it cleared off beautifully, and I went on deck and enjoyed the many strange scenes that are ever happening in harbor and on shore. I have had every good thing to eat this day you can think of. It has been since the first of last September since we had fresh meat to eat.

Capt. Rose and wife of the *National Eagle*[V] came on board and we are all to go ashore tomorrow.

February 13th. A beautiful, beautiful day and I dress to go on shore, but I do not remember what I wore. I shall have to refer you to my wardrobe as described previously for you to judge what you think would be the most suitable costume.

Father went on board the *National Eagle* to survey[G] her. Her crew had mutined and would not go to sea on her.

When he returned he had Capts. Rose and Mitchell with him, and Mrs. Rose had sent me a half dozen bottles of beer and said she would go ashore after dinner.

At one o'clock we started.

There is only one gate by which you can enter the city, and we had to pass through two walls before we got into the city streets. At this last wall a strong guard is stationed. We went up to the ship chandlers, Mr. Molineaux, where a guide and interpreter joined us.

We took a cab and had a nice long ride, rising higher all the time until we reached a big gate. Here we left the cab, and the interpreter tried to find some jackasses for us to ride, but could only get three so we decided to walk. As we passed through the gate, the soldiers, for here also was a strong guard, told us to look upon the rocks over head, and such a sight of monkeys great and small, smooth and wrinkled, jabbering and jumping as free as air.

It has never been learned where these monkeys came from, for they entirely disappear for a part of the year and no one has been able to find out where they go or whence they come.

The only way that has suggested itsalf is in a subterranean channel under the straits, to the coast of Africa. There is nothing for them to eat and so the government feeds them.

Then we entered the great fort. At first it was very dark, but we got use to walking in these long channels, cut through the sold rock. The darkness is relieved at intervals by port holes, where immense guns are mounted.

I do not see how such immense guns were ever placed in position.

It took one hundred mules to draw them up to where they were mounted. Then we went out and took a view of the land "neutral," a strange piece of natural land that separates the rock from Spain. It was so flat I should think the seas would wash completely over it.

We are six hundred and seventy-nine feet above sea level and looked over the towns of Spain and saw an immense bull ring that had just been completed, but we did not see a bull fight for it was out of season.

The vessels look like row boats, and still we climb up higher and enter another part of the fort called "St. George Hall."

It was semi-circular and had five great guns mounted. I got up and looked through one of the port holes, and hundreds of feet, perpendicularly below me was solid rock.

No person could scale such a wall, while at the foot was the blue Mediterranean, and I saw my first "Felucca,"[G] a boat peculiar to these countries, but so picturesque.

On our way down we passed an old Moorish Castle that had been built nine hundred and fifty years, and was the Moors' stronghold when they crossed the straits and into Spain.

After we reached town we went to a coffee house and had refreshments, and then came on board, tired but feeling well repaid for all our exertions.

I somehow felt that I was to see strange sights as I had read a great deal about Spain and "Dago"[G] countries.

I visited Mrs. Rose on her vessel. She gave me three pairs of kid gloves. I was blessed with a small hand. We went on shore and wandered through the streets and into the stores, and looked into the windows.

It is father's fifty-fifth birthday. His eyes are still troubling him; I bought him a reading glass for a birthday present. Mrs. Rose was quite provoked because her husband did not come on shore, and said he should not have any beer when she got back. He is a German, and she is an Austrian, and both are just as nice as can be.

The gentlemen call about the fleet evenings, but if they are out after nine P. M. they may get challenged by the police boat.

February 15th. Bound for the summit of Gibralter rock.

Mrs. Rose, Mr. Whitmore. an interpreter and myself left the city in a cab after dinner. After a nice ride they brought along four jackasses, two saddled for gentlemen and two for ladies. I shall never forget the scene. Mr. Whitmore's feet nearly touched the ground. If father had come his would have dragged. The ladies had a frame around them and a foot rest. The jackasses were led by boys and so near the edge of the foot path would they go I thought many times that we would surely fall over the edge. This was indeed an experience. I surely have been well repaid for my determination to go to sea. But what a scene! Way up in the air! The beautiful Mediterranean before us. Africa's coast abeam, and Spain behind.

The sky was perfectly beautiful, while beyond the Spanish coast was a long range of snow capped mountains, blue and silver, so fascinating one wanted to reach out and take them.

It did not seem natural, rather fairy like.

When we were about two-thirds up the hill we stopped at a large hole in the rock and dismounted. We were at the mouth of a large cave. We entered and a soldier lighted some candles for us, and we started to explore. Down a flight of stone steps, around corners, through narrow passages and then the interpreter lighted a blue light and told us to look around.

Innumerable stalactites hung from an immense dome and great stalagmites rose from the very bottom to the top. They looked like light brown rice. We passed through another small opening and found ourselves in another immense chamber. On the side was a spring of water where we quenched out thirst. The water was as cold as ice. Across the cave we were conveyed to a small opening about as large as the head of a hogshead, but were warned not to go through, but were allowed to throw stones. The mysteries of this place have never been solved. Two men who went in were never seen or heard from again. No cry reached out, no sound of body falling. Shoutings and hundreds of feet of rope availed nothing.

There was never a bottom found. The popular idea at that time was, that it was a subterranean passage to Africa. The story as told was so gruesome I was glad to get away. As we returned and reached the last cave we looked up and in the opening ahead that revealed light was one of the jackasses, so completely outlined against the sky, it was a funny sight.

Coming out of the cave we again mounted and started for the top, arriving there at 4 P.M.

We went to the top of the signal station and two soldiers placed me on top of the highest gun.

We were nearly fifteen hundred feet above the sea level.

I could look over Spain and see two rivers very plainly; one had quite a large island in it.

Many different towns could also be seen here and there. After a rest and enjoyable time looking about over the sea, Straits, bay, Spain, Africa, and thanking the soldiers for their kindness, we started for the city. As we descended the first thing I knew there was nothing below me but fog, as it seemed to me. The sky was clear above and I thought I was to dash into a cold stream, but the interpreter told me we were above the clouds, and sure enough, a large cloud had settled below us and cut the view off, but it soon moved on and everything seemed natural again. It was a most peculiar sensation, like soap-suds.

We were an hour coming down and had lunch at a coffee house and then came on board, tired as I could be but elated over my trip.

The sixteenth found the mate real sick and father not very well, so I remained on board all day and cared for them. Read, entertained callers and walked deck.

We bought four pins of a man who came on board to

sell jewelry to the sailors. The pins were of silver and Gibralter rock.

During the early morning a boat came along side and brought us letters and a telegram from Paris, France, to proceed to Barcelona, Spain, to discharge. These letters had been sent to Valparaiso, and were so late getting there that we missed them and they were remailed.

After dinner I went ashore for father was very miserable, and up to the American consul's, Mr. Sprague, to attend to some business for father. I went in a carriage, and after Mr. Sprague had attended to the business he took me about the house which was perfectly lovely. Such a beautiful conservatory I never was in before. He loaded me down with the most beautiful violets, and good wishes, when I left. Then I went into the stores awhile and down to the ship chandler's, who gave me two bottles of cologne. I went up stairs to meet his wife and a lady friend, who did everything in their power to give me a good time. They invited me to a ball and served a splendid dinner, and loaded me down with good things when I left. I came on board at 6 P. M. and we shall go to sea tomorrow morning.

February 19th, as soon as daylight we got under way and out to sea. After we got back of the rock it was like dodging a bumble bee. Thirty-two vessels awaiting a fair wind to go through the Straits. The current runs out and never in. One can get out with a calm as the swift current will carry them out, but a fair wind must be had to get in.

I am overwhelmed with fruit and luxuries of all kinds.

Such dates I never believed could grow! Almost as large as lemons.

Father is very miserable and nearly blind. I made a shade for him today, but do not know what else to do for him. If he does not get help in Barcelona he will have to leave the ship.

It is a delightful sail. The sunrise over the snow capped mountains was something indescribable.

Every hill has a watch tower or light house on it.

We pass Cape de Gata^G today and are making fine headway. I cannot afford to miss any of this scenery, every foot of which is just beautiful, and I am on deck from daybreak until late at night. We can see the towns and villages all along the shore. After four days sail, we make Barcelona, but it is night and no breeze, so we lay off awaiting the coming day.

The trip has been delightful, full of pretty scenes, and many kinds of sailing craft.

The next day at six A. M. we head for the harbor and a tug took us at eight, and at nine, we dropped anchors just within the breakwater.

'The Spanish bugle
is so sweet and its tones come over
the water so beautifully.'

Chapter Fifteen

BARCELONA

There are more brokers around in this port than any where we have arrived at, and just the moment the officer left the ship they flocked on board and completely filled the cabin, and part of the deck. It took some time for all to say their say and at last all was quiet and I went on deck to look round. A fine city I see, beautiful streets, lighted with electric lights, hills, mountains. Handsome club boats come and go; one had fourteen oars pulling.

We have a custom house officer on board, who is to

Barcelona, Rambla de las Flores. (The Boston Atheneum)

remain until we are discharged.

The Spaniards have lots of red tape, even our sugar sealed up, and we are only allowed just a little out to use and when we want more an officer has to come and open the seal.

I saw a fashion plate today on the roof of a boat house just astern. As a large steamer was going out sea, seven young dandies came out and lined up to watch the steamer and they looked just like a fashion plate. We are moored to a quay or breakwater and have two hawsers out astern. This afternoon a young fellow in stiff hat was running along under the hawsers and his hat got knocked off and he said: "Rompei Cabaza," break my head. Of course I laughed and he thumbed his nose at me.

A young clerk from the firm we are consigned called and spent the evening. He was very pleasant. Feb. 20th, I remained on board all day long and the custom house officer's wife was on board. Of course I could not talk to her or she to me, but I showed her different books and pictures, and enjoyed hearing her talk to herself, and managed to wear the day away, The weather is simply beautiful, every thing so blue and silvery.

I go on shore to see a procession. Four figures of Christ borne on the shoulders of young men, a band of music, a band of priests, and candles enough to light up all out doors.

The ladies and gentlemen in "turnouts" were "stunning." They were dressed very nicely and the gentlemen on horseback were fine.

I do not think the Spanish ladies so very handsome, as I have always heard that they were. The handsomest one I every saw was in a row boat with three other women, about the vessel shouting to the sailors, and especially calling for "Bender,"[G] who was a "black niggar."

Then we went through the market where one always finds funny things, and new things. One lady comes in and buys a live hen. The market woman kills and dresses it right there, puts the entrails in to a drawer under her bench[.] Up along comes a low class woman and buys the entrails and takes them home. I did not ask for an invitation to dinner.

A Mr. and Mrs. Butler came on board and took me up town to do some shopping. I bought a pair of French kid boots, laced up inside with a blue silk cord, and then buttoned over. They were the best fitting shoes I ever had and kept their shape splendidly.

Silk and cotton goods are not cheaper than at home.

We went into the Public Gardens, and, oh horrors! I had my first experience with beggars.

At the gate were a man and woman and two children. The children were blind and carried musical instruments, but such eyes, I never saw. Wide open but covered with a white substance that made them look so repulsive. They came up to me and of course I gave them some money. Mrs. Butler says that probably their parents put their eyes out to get a living by them. I only wish I had made a complete list of all the beggars I saw in Barcelona alone. Every few steps you came upon something on the ground in front of you. One of the worst was a man facing me but his legs were out behind him and he walked up to me with his hands, dragging his legs, with his feet sticking up. Such twisted, blind, sick looking creatures at every turn.

The gardens were like all Public and Botanical gardens, rare fruit, flowers and trees, all well kept. A date tree took my eye, also the dandy dressed men promaneding about. The Spanish men are the best dressed of any I ever saw[.] So lazy also saucy.

We came on board to dinner and after tea, had a dance on board and a general good time.

I missed this morning, for the first time since we came into port, the soldiers who drill for an hour every morning just outside the city on a hill.

The Spanish bugle is so sweet and its tones come over the water so beautifully. I have never been able to tell why that bugle call impressed me so. I can even hear it now and see those bugles shine in the sun.

We dock, and I go ashore with Mr. and Mrs. Butler. It is Sunday and we go to an immense Cathedral, hundreds of years old. Went into a room where bishops and priests are

Barcelona Cathedral. (The Boston Atheneum)

buried, and candles burn all the time for them. It was damp and cold. We passed into the principal part of the church and it was simply bewildering! I had never seen such beautiful things.

Stained glass windows, and the ceiling of the church was an immense painting. I do not see how anyone could paint over head at such a height. It was so high it seemed uncanny. The place of the crucifixion was beautiful and such ornaments adorned it!

We saw a crowd and some one asked what was going on. Some one said: "A christening," so we looked on. Fourteen little babies only a few hours old, and dressed in the most elegant clothes.

As they formed a circle, the babies in the arms of their nurses, a priest in the center, followed by a small boy in red, with a yellow regalia over his neck, some one threw a handful of beans into one of the babies faces and set it to crying.

First the priest went around and breathed on the babies, said something and crossed them, then he rubbed something across their lips that looked like rock salt, said some more Spanish and crossed them again, all the time the small boy was following him, chewing something as energetically as an American girl chews gum; and would squeal out something that sounded like "Amen."

After this the nurses took off the babies' clothes and they were taken up to an immense silver bowl and with what looked like an overgrown soup ladle the priest baptised them, another priest anointed them and then all was over, except some one opened a bottle of beer in the crowd, and when the cork came out you would almost think a bomb had exploded. The church was dark and gloomy for all the candles that were burning. There were so many peasants there in corduory clothes that the air was simply dreadful. We went to a cafe for refreshments and then on board.

In the evening an American called who lived in Dexter, Maine. He was the mate of the English steamer *Ceto* and was like "home folks." After all the company had gone we had some bread and cheese, and went to bed with plenty to think about.

Fine weather and I entertained myself with some Spanish women who came on board out of curiosity to see the vessel, and I showed them about and treated them on ship's bread and American cheese.

At four P. M. Mr. Sutherland, a ship chandler, his wife and two little girls, aged seven and nine years, called.

They are English people and I was much pleased with them. I am to go to their house to dinner tomorrow. After tea, father and I took a walk on shore for awhile, went to a cafe and had bread, cheese and beer and then returned.

Mr. Sutherland called to take me up to his house to dinner. They live in a flat and are very comfortable.

We had a nice dinner, after which Mrs. Sutherland and I went on a shopping trip. I bought an olive green dress and satin to trim it with, and then we went to a dressmaker's to have it made. I think I shall like the dress very much. I returned on board to tea, and in the evening the captain and mate of the *Ceto* called and we all went up town for awhile, after which we came home to our evening repast and to rest.

March 5th was unpleasant but Mrs. Sutherland came down and we went to the dressmaker's to try on the dress and it was all right.

I bought me some new hose, white cotton with a red vine running up the leg of one pair, and blue dots up the other pair. Quite a set off to my already overstocked wardrobe, and then when I arrived home my sisters made fun of them.

Then we went into a church. I thought I had seen the best one but this was "more so." All of gilt and paintings. The organ was grand! Services going on all the time. Today father has tried Mr. Sutherland's doctor and I do hope he will improve.

March 6th. Another nasty, disagreeable day. I go up the "Rambla"G and exercise my Spanish at an apothecary shop. Got what I wanted after a while, but I dare to venture a goodly sum that those clerks had a good laugh after I went out. We learned to day of the arrival at Valencia of the *Eyvor,*V Capt. Atkins, and also that he had to go to Port Mahone for quarantine for ten days. It is a shame for now we shall not see him.

March 9th. Pleasant once more and I went up to Mrs. Sutherland's alone. One nicely dressed "gentleman" shouted out something, but I went right along. Mrs. Sutherland said I ought not to come alone. I feel like a fool taking a man or servant to protect me in broad daylight.

I met with a Capt. Robinstrom and sister and they were all going to ride, and insisted that I go with them.

They had a fine pair of bays and an open carriage and a driver with a cockade in his hat. We rode out in the country which is green and nice now, and stopped at a church.

One room where everything given to the Virgin is, was crowded full.

The ceiling hangs with wax models of hands, feet, arms, legs, busts, noses, ears, heads, cases where if the Virgin would cure them of certain ailments they give a model of that member of the church.

There were some beautiful heads of hair hanging upon the wall, and one soldier had given his whole costume. He had promised the Virgin that if she would bring him home from the war all safe he would give his uniform.

A great many pictures lined the walls.

Vessels at sea in terrible storms, and the waves beating over them, their masts and sails gone, and the row boats bottom up with men hanging to them. Pictures of a great many explosions. One factory, the side blown out, and women falling to the ground in all attitudes.

In one picture of a steamer exploding is a woman over the quarter rail, head down, and all that holds her is a hoop skirt.

A man is falling from a four-story building on to an iron fence; but the one that took my eye was, a chamber with a woman on the bed and three doctors are performing an operation on her. One doctor holds her pulse, one is cutting open her side with something that looks like a razor, and the third is holding a large wash bowl for the blood to run into. No one seems to be giving the ether.

There is a life-size image of the Savior here. It is his real body. It was found floating in some Spanish bay and brought here.

Long black hair, straight and dark hangs from his head, and blood is apparently dropping from his side, hands and feet. The crown of thorns was not washed off by the waves, but still adorns his head, and the blood is dropping from his forehead.

Once a year he weeps tears of blood, some one goes behind the image and squeezes blood from a sponge so it drops from his eyes. This is a custom of great matter and crowds come each year to see it.

I cannot begin to tell one-half that I saw. After going

over the entire church we returned home. In the evening Mr. Whitmore and myself went up into the city for while; went to a cafe and had a cream and home again. Mr. Whitmore speaks Spanish so we can get about anywhere.

Mrs. Sutherland, three children and servant come down and stay all day, and such a good time as those children had, swinging, climbing the rigging and fishing. It was a gala day for them and they did not want to go home when night came.

Father and I walked up home with them and then we went over the city.

My new dress came home today. It cost me sixteen dollars and is pretty nice. I like it the best of any dress I ever had.

I got up at six and went to the market place before breakfast. It is eel day and such heaps of eels as are seen everywhere.

After breakfast the American consul called, and after dinner, Mrs. Butler, followed soon by a Norwegian and an Austrian Captain. At three we all went up into the Public Gardens and Park.

It is ever so pretty and the fountains are magnificent.

There is a small natural cave, some deer and monkeys, and fine music. We walked around among the people and came down on board the vessel at six o'clock, and the steward had not commenced to get supper; so I asked the mate to go out and see what was the matter. He returned and said the steward was drunk, but would get us some supper. I waited an hour and went out myself, and he had a spider half full of water, with several slices of fat salt port floating around, and no fire in the stove.

So I told him not to bother. I built a fire and made some tea and we had a cold supper.

Mr. Whitemore and I went up town to a cafe for cream, and to hear the music. It was a large orchestra and played finely. When we returned, we found Capt. Sorensen on board with father, and as we all have very bad colds we put cayenne pepper in the beer, and if the captain was not cured it was not for the lack of pepper in the bottom of his glass. I did not intend to burn him up. My intentions were good.

A walk up the "Rambla" is of quite an interest to me because of the lovely costumes of the ladies, and the dandy dressed men. They surely are worth seeing.

I received a visit from the Sutherland children. They stayed all day and nearly unrigged the ship, and jumped and screamed, but they were happy and that is a good deal. They stayed to tea, and after they went home I wrote letters and fought the nimble flea.

Arrangements were made with Mr. and Mrs. Butler to go into the country tomorrow, so I shall have to rise early. We went up town for some necessary articles, and some medicine for father, who is improving very much under the doctor's care.

We take a long walk, and each time see a new part of the city.

I got up at quarter past five this morning to go out into the country. At eight Mr. and Mrs. Butler, father and myself took the steam cars out of the city, traveling very fast. We passed the stronghold of the city, which was a very large building, and had a fearfully high tower. This stronghold has no doors or windows near the ground, but possibly thirty feet up was a door. We passed a large building that had four towers on it, and it was from these towers that they watched the mountains for any approach of the enemy. We rode close to the seashore and the scenery was fine.

The place we went to was called "Bardalona,"[G] a small fishing town, and the long fish nets were all laid out on the beach.

We went to a country house, up one flight from the goats, cows and mules that were underneath. Here we sampled some most delicious wine, the pure juice of the grape.

We had a nice call and then went to the church.

The work in one country church costs more than in a dozen of ours. They must have had a great many ten cent socials to pay for such structures as these, if that is the way their money was raised.

We visited a cousin of Mrs. Butler's and there we had a graham bread, sausages roasted on a pointed stick over a charcoal fire, and wine.

In the Public Square was a large stone trough of water and seven women were washing their clothes and pounding them with great big wooden paddles.

The tub had been built for two hundred years and was actually worn by pounding.

We called upon an uncle of Mr. Butler's and I had such aching eyes I could not keep them open, they smarted so. A gentleman gave me a basin of water and a towel, and I bathed them for awhile and they felt better. Here we had some more bread and wine. Then we went to a cafe and had some soda water, and bought three rabbits to take home with us, and left them with friends, and went to dinner. After which we went to a gentleman's garden that was fine.

The grounds had very large orchards of orange trees in them, and the grounds were laid out beautifully. Large ponds of water, a stream running through, a boat in the stream, and a bridge over it, but the prettiest part was the grotto carved out of natural stone.

Up to the top was a girl and a boy under an umbrella, and below them a bridge, while on either sides was an old castle, below the bridge was a windmill, and on either side were shepards with their sheep, while under all was a lion and more boys and girls.

A swing on a merry-go-round, a gift of branches loaded with oranges, pears and more oranges, and it was time to go home.

We went and got the rabbits, and Mrs. Butler hung them over her arm, and put my shawl over them, thus smuggling them through the gates, otherwise we would have had to pay duty on them, but the great officers of the train would not allow them in our car, so they had to go to the freight car and we had to pay freight on them.

We arrived on board at seven, and after serving supper Mr. and Mrs. Butler went home and I found my bed and I was indeed a tired girl.

March 17th. This afternoon I went up to Mrs. Sutherland's and got her to go with me to the photographers for the proofs of my pictures[G], and I took them with me to show father. We did some sho[p]ping, then we went back to Mrs. Sutherland's to tea, and during the evening played games.

I waited until ten for Mr. Sutherland to come home to go home with me. Mrs. Sutherland would not let me go alone. At half past twelve he arrived but then they thought it too late so we had another supper and talked until two in the morning.

We did not rise very early this morning and at ten I started to go on board the vessel. I met Capt. Sorenson and he said the vessel had hauled out into the harbor, so he went up to the photographers with me and I ordered the pictures, then we went into the Gardens for a while, then to a cafe to dinner, and he left me at Mrs. Sutherland's.

At five P. M. I came on board the vessel, and had been away over twenty-four hours, the longest time since I first came on board. Mr. Fallon, the clerk, came on board and staid the evening. He brought a lot of reading and took a letter to Capt. Atkins at Valencia, as he was going there the next day.

March 19th. On board all day and the vessel just rolling and tossing. Mrs. Sutherland and the children came on board. She was quite sick but the children were not still long enough.

For two days I remained on board busy with chronometer time and rating, for we are to go to sea in a few days, and I want to know how the time is.

The U. S. consul came on board and shipped three men and made a nice call.

The twenty-second was a long day. Settling up father's accounts came first, after which I went on shore and got my pictures and did some final shopping and took dinner at Mrs. Sutherland's.

When I arrived on board I found the mate had fallen into the hold, and although no bones were broken, for which I was truly thankful, he was badly wrenched and lame.

The cabin soon filled up with captains, and at four P. M. we all went on shore and took a long walk. Supper at a cafe and on board for the evening, and a jolly evening it was, even if we were never to see each other again.

It does seem queer to meet these good friends and then part forever, without a thought or sorrow, and scarcely a regret.

March 23rd and we are ready for sea. I was up bright and early with my work all done, so as to be at liberty to say good bye to all callers.

The Butlers, Capt. Sorensen and Mr. Sutherland came.

At nine A. M. the tug had us at sea.

No wind, so we lazily drift away. At dark Barcelona is just visible, and after dark her many electric lights make the sky look like Northern Lights.

The steamer *Castlefond*,[V] Capt. Rhinstrom left today for Tarragona, and the *Souviner*,[V] Capt. Sorensen, leaves tomorrow.

I had a most delightful time at Barcelona and now look forward to our arrival at Tarapina,[G] Sicely, where we are going in ballast[G] to load salt for Rockland, Maine.

*'I do not lack for flowers.
I have thirteen large bouquets
on hand. . .'*

Chapter Sixteen

POND SAILING AND TRAPANI

Mediterranean sailing is fascinating. Father calls it pond sailing for land is in sight all th[e] time.

First the Island of Minorca, then the coast of Africa, next the Island of Sardinia where we sail almost up into the harbor of Cagliari[G] and see the town which is very odd looking. I feel as if I would like to go ashore there, then we tack for the shore of Tunis[.] The winds are against us and we are just beating back and forth, and gain what we can.

On March 29th a heavy gale appears, and we lay to

for sixteen hours, and we are right under the land at Sardinia.

The wind came fair, also the weather. I do not try to accomplish anything only watch the shores and craft, and navigate a little. It is interesting now to study the chart for all the landmarks, islands, soundings, etc.

April 1st the island of Sicely is in sight and all is excitement; a fair wind and prospects of arriving at Trapani,[G] and sure enough at half after seven P. M., in the dark, we drop anchor at Trapani in the midst of a medly of children crying and a band playing.

A broker came along side and the pilot staid all night. I am anxious for morning so I can see what the place looks like.

Trapani and Rodilico! I got up early to see the sights, but Mr. Rodilico got up before me, and was on board before I got out of my stateroom.

When I appeared, I found Mr. Rodilico, the Captain of the Port, a Custom House official, with four attendants. Quite a family.

We at once hauled into the quay and father went on shore to enter his vessel.

Such a queer looking town and Mr. Rodilico has promised to take us all around. Fifty-three church[es] here, and nunneries galore!

At four P. M. father came on board and asked me would I go to ride, and of course I said "Yes." A gentleman with a most beautiful carriage and horses came down to the vessel and took father, Mr. Rodilico and myself out into the country to a fine house with beautiful grounds.

We had plenty of wine, flowers, oranges, lemons and plums.

There was a small girl out there as fleshy and dark as

my sister Annie, both father and I noticed how much they looked alike.

Mr. Rodilico has taken three meals on board today and bought me a bottle of goat's milk, and to cap the climax, he called again at half past eight and brought me another bouquet, which makes three, this is surely a good beginning.

In spite of all my endeavors to rise before Mr. Rodilico came, he out ran me, and got here before I was dressed, and staid to breakfast, and at ten came and took us up town sight seeing.

First a church, as wonderful as any I had seen at Barcelona, marble carvings, and one room of wood carvings, also a room of models to the Virgin.

Then we went to a nunnery and had a talk with some nuns, and bought some of their cake and candy. One woman asked if father was my husband. Father asked her where hers was and she held up a small crucifix and said she was wedded to that. Then we went to see them make maccaroni. There is a large wheel like a mill wheel and this kneads dough in a large trough, then this dough is pressed through a large cylinder with a perforated bottom, the dough is forced through by a heavy weight pressed down by a hand screw.

After fanning it for awhile it is cut off and hung over bamboo sticks to dry. It can be handled like a lot of wrapping twine.

We went on board for dinner and staid the rest of the day, but in the evening a band came down on the quay and played. I always thought Mr. Rodilico got them to come down.

He is a funny fellow, not bad looking, with a drawling voice, a good heart and a persistency that will last a life

Marine salt works at Trapani. (From Will S. Monroe, 'Sicily, the Garden of the Mediterraneum'. Boston: L.C. Page & Co. 1909)

time. He has certainly given us a fine time this day.

Away in a carriage in the afternoon to the salt pans.[G] Five hundred windmills pump water from the Mediterranean sea into large pans of earth, where the sun evaporates the water, and after all the process is over the salt is as white as snow. This was a funny sensation for we were below the surface of the Medeterranean and the vessels all looked above us.

These salt pans run way down the coast to Ma[r]sala, where a delicious wine is made, just sour enough.

I had a great run in the fields. One pretty sight was a large field of ripened poppies.

Above Trapani on the top of a high mauntain is the City of St. Julian,[G] said to have been built before Christ. You will hear more of it later.

In the evening we took a walk up town and went into a few stores and into a place called a Passion House. Here are a great many images representing Christ while on earth.

"Christ suffering on the cross," "the Jews stripping him," "Where he is taken down and laid out," and many others. Women are kissing their fingers and touching the image, and then letting the children kiss their hands, but I felt the climax had been reached when one woman took hold of Jesus' toe and shook it. I had to laugh. She looked daggers at me, and I guess was pretty mad, but it was a funny sight. After this, we called at a lady's home, she and a lady friend were smoking cigarettes, and were much surprised to think father and I did not smoke. She promised to take us to her country seat tomorrow. After all this, we went to a cafe, had ice cream, and went home.

At twelve, the lady came with a most beautiful carriage; navy blue linings and snail pearl trimmings, and we rode for an hour, way out in a beautiful country, and to her country home, We had cake and wine served out of doors at a table under a large tree, whose trunk was completely-surrounded with a bed of black pansies, the largest and blackest I ever saw; just like velvet.

We had four bottles of wine given us, that was sixty years old, oranges, lemons, plums, flowers from sorts of plants, and a pair of handsome white doves with pink feet. I do not remember the lady's name. Her husband was an Algerian, and she said her son would come and call on me, and sure enough after we got back, if Mr. Rodilico did not, an hour later, present to me a large black curly headed young man, who bent his knee and kissed my hand and presented me with a bouquet he could scarcely get through the door, with a beautiful flower in the center called a carmelion.

I nearly collapsed as I was not used to such attention, and I nearly laughed aloud when I saw that grinning father of mine taking it all in.

Nevertheless he was a very nice young man and I enjoyed his call very much.

In the evening Capt. Romus, of the Norwegian steamer *Amicitia*,[v] Mr. Rodilico, father, Mr. and Mrs. Burgarella and myself went to the theatre, and as ladies never go into the pit but always have a box, here was a grand chance to air my Japanese silk dress, and mother's old bonnet strings which I did to good advantage, as I was given the seat of honor in the box, that commanded the entrance to the theatre, and not the stage. I do not wonder so many glasses were turned my way, but I always thought, and do now, that they were looking at Mrs. Burgarella, who was very handsome, and dark, and she had beautiful red poppies in her hair and a handsome grey dress trimmed with black lace.

The play was Russian, and of course I did not understand it, but enjoyed my evening very much nevertheless.

Got home at twelve and to bed at one, to get up at four A. M., April 6th, to go up a mountain to a place called St. Julian. There were only two seats in the coach and each seat would hold three, but Mr. Burgarella had paid for all six seats, so we should have plenty of room.

Capt. Romus, Mr. Rodilico, father and I went into the coach.

It took three hours to reach the top. We had to travel zig-zig, it was so steep.

The mountain is two thousand, four hundred feet high.

We went to see the old walls and old gate of the city.

Three churches with immense stone pillars. I do not see how so much material was ever carried up there. They claim that the city was built before Christ. It surely is a very ancient looking place.

We saw an old castle, now used for a prison, and the view from here was perfectly beautiful and fascinating. What seemed to be hills from the vessel we could look over and around, and see miles and miles of country. The view of the salt pans down the coast was very curious, and the Mediterranean from this point cannot be described.

We went to an old well that was completely covered with green ivy. It was sacred for some reason, but I have forgotten now what it was.

We were followed by a crowd of men, women and children, who thought father was a giant.

The walls were covered with hieroglyphics and they asked if father could read them, and he said "Yes" and explained how the city happened to be built was, that at the time of the flood, Noah's oldest son got mad and stole the long boat of the Ark and ran away with his wife and landed on top of this hill, just sticking out of the water, and finally this city grew up.

We went to a hotel to dinner and had macarroni and boneless chicken. The macarroni I did not like and as for the chicken[,] it was a skin filled with mushy stuff and squares of fat pork and ham pressed into it, and the only chicken found was on Capt. R[o]mus' plate, and I reached for it with my fork. We fought over it, finally he ran around the dining room and I after him. There were four students at a table and they thought it was a fight and commenced to take my part, finally I ate the chicken, but was sorry afterwards. We arrived home at six P. M. and were two hours coming down, but it was a fine experience.

Mr. Rodilico eats on the vessel, and I guess sleeps on the ship's hawser, for he cannot go far he gets back so quickly in the morning.

An American barkentine *Mercidita*,[v] Capt. Preston, arrived in port and the captain came on board during the evening, and by the time all had said good bye I was glad to recognize my bed.

The forenoon was used up in receiving callers and making lemon pies which I hope will be good for the Captains are coming to tea this evening.

I am sorry to have to say that this is Capt. Romus' last evening, as he sails tomorrow.

We had a fine supper; the pies were all right.

Mr. Whitmore came in and joined us. Mr. Rodilico was of an inquiring turn of mind, so he turned to Capt. Romus and said, in his drawling tone of voice:

"Capt.! what is the cause of an explosion?"

"The boiler bursts," says Capt. Romus.

"No, but what is the cause of an explosion?" says Mr. Rodilico, emphasizing the cause.

"Sometimes the cylinder head blows out?" says the Capt.

"No! but what is the cause of an explosion," says Mr. Rodilico, still emphasizing the cause.

Father speaks up and says:

"Sometimes wind and sometimes beans."

This was enough. Mr. Whitmore looked disgusted.

Capt. Preston looked as if he would explode.

Capt. R[o]mus tried to look innocent, and I had business in the dining cabin.

After all had calmed down, Mr. Rodilico drawled out:

"Miss Atwood, did you ever hear the opera 'Margarite?'"[G]

"No, I never had."

Then he asked several more and he received the same answer.

Finally father asked:

"Mr. Rodilico, did you ever hear the opera, 'Cat tracks out of the ash hole?'"

"No," Mr. Rodilico drawled out, "but I would like to, also some of the American songs that were so popular."

Capt. Preston and I went on deck to rest our faces, mine was actually in pain, trying to keep sober.

At last we had to say good bye to Capt. Romus, as he was to leave at daybreak.

At three thirty P. M., I go on shore with Mr. Rodilico to do some shopping. A silk umbrella for three dollars, a half a dozen pairs of gloves for two dollars and forty cents.

Then we went to a large wine cellar. Such immense casks. The[re] must have been hogsheads of wine in them, and there were dozens of them; some were twelve feet ab[o]ve father's head, and we had a great sampling time, after which we all returned to the bark for the evening.

The next day a lady sent me down a basket of oranges and an invitation to ride out into the country, which I accepted and was treated sumptuously and returned loaded down with lemons, plums, green almonds, strawberries and flowers. This was my first experience with champagne, and it was a most delightful one. As we were walking through the garden, a bee stung father on his ear, and that member became quite painful.

The ladies will visit the bark tomorrow. I fix up everything very nice to entertain them. I do not lack for flowers. I have thirteen large bouquets on hand, and I have to shut them in the washroom at night they are so fragrant, and last night I pitched four large ones onto the deck of the *Mercedita* for I had no place to put them.

Mr. Rodilico says: "The ladies do not like to go on board the vessels they are so dirty."

Their surprise was great when they arrived at two P. M.— every deck, mast, floor and cabin white and cleaner than their own homes.

Two ladies and two gentlemen called, and later on four more gentlemen.

We had ship's bread, American cheese and wine and they staid about two hours.

After tea we all went on shore to see a procession. It was an alter with the Virgin Mary on one side and the head of Jesus on the other, carried by four men and followed by a band of music and a large crowd, mostly women.

This is Easter season and the churches are draped about the altars with the most beautiful lace and silk and embroidered draperies I ever saw.

We have been in fifteen churches today.

Mr. Whitmore and I went on shore and visited eighteen different churches and had some cream at a cafe before we came home. The rest of the day I received callers and entertained Mr. Rodilico.

After tea Mr. Burgarella and wife called and with father, Mr. Rodilico and myself we went on shore to Mr. Burgarella's office, where we had fine seats on a balcony to see a parade.

Such a crowd! Barnum's circus would not compare. The parade was led by a band, followed by about forty small boys decorated with gold chains and carrying candles, these were followed by about forty young men carrying candles. Then an image^G carried by four men made on a platform of white material representing "Christ taking leave of his mother," between each image were boys and young men and now and then a band. The second image, "Christ finds the deciples sleeping and chides them" third, "Jesus was being bound and Judas was betraying him," then followed: "Christ smote by the High Priest," "Peter striking off the Priest's ear," "Peter's denial of Christ and the cock crowing," "and the maid by the fire," "Jesus before Pilate," "The soldiers scourging Jesus," "Cutting Jesus' hair off," "Jesus before Herod," "Pilate washing his hands and showing he was through with the matter," "Jesus being stripped of his clothing[,]" "Binding Jesus to the cross," "Jesus was nailed to the cross and it was being raised," "The soldiers were piercing Jesus' side," "Jesus was taken down from the cross and his mother was with him," "they roll him in a shroud," "Jesus in his coffin," and last "the Virgin Mary." The parade lasted from half past six P. M. until three A. M.

It was twelve o'clock before we saw the last part and got on board the vessel. We went into no churches today.

April 12th. A beautiful world to awaken in. Every thing is ablaze.

At nine the lady of the beautifull carriage came and took us to an old temple and monastery to see the ascension of Christ.

A large curtain covered the altar at the church. The church was packed to suffocation with people of all classes. Birds were flying about the church and the air was full of confetti.

At about half past ten the cord was cut that held the curtain, and as the curtain fell a life-sized figure of Christ was seen to ascend and disappear into the clouds and such shouting and pounding was never heard.

After ascension, we went over the temple and monastery where the old monks used to live, over their kitchen, dining room and sleeping rooms, and then we waited for the unveiling of the Virgin.

The throng was so dense that my hostess asked permission to step within the first veil that concealed the Virgin from sight and it was granted. So we had a nice chance.

When the first veil was drawn the crowds shouted and pounded so, I could not think what had happened, but when the second veil was drawn it was simply belum [bedlam].

But what a sight!

A beautiful life-sized figure of the Virgin[G] in alabaster with the child Jesus on her arm. She was bedecked from the crown of her head to the sole of her foot with jewels. Her fingers were loaded with costly rings that beggar description. I counted twelve watches and chains on her and the crown on her head was a diadem beyond description. There must have been represented thousands of dollars.

These gifts had all been given for services rendered by the Virgin. The lady with me had promised her diamonds to her if she would save the life of her daughter who was hurt in a run away, but as she died the lady was still wearing her diamonds. After we returned home and had dinner we all went to another ascension but was nothing to what I had seen in the forenoon.

A band of music was in the church and as it started to play a lot of birds were let loose to represent the ascension. Here again was a great crowd but we were lucky to be near the door.

On board to tea, and in the evening Capt. Preston joined us and we went up to one of the Mr. Burgarella's to spend the evening.

I wondered where we were going. We went into a door and passed horses and carriages and nut bins, up a flight of stairs, and were received with open arms into a most magnificent parlor and were right royally entertained.

Sunday, Capt. Preston and I went on a long walk along the promenade, and at the end was the city's stronghold like all the rest we had seen with towers and the doors way up where only a very long ladder could reach. After our return the captain staid the day with us and in the evening we all went to a dance. Mr. Rodilico had asked a gentleman from out of town to sing for me. He did so very nicely, and another gentleman sang a song on fireworks and acted it out, and it was laughable enough. I had three offers to dance from officers in uniform, but did not accept and we only staid a little while. As we were coming home we met Mr. and Mrs. Burgarella and took a walk about the city.

Such funny streets, so narrow and the buildings are so high, and no windows next to the street in the nunneries. We go to the nunneries quite often to talk. We have to talk through bars and there is a funny looking affair that looks like a barrel; it turns around and one side of it is open so you can put in any gift you want to for them. I carried some hardbread one day and the nun was delighted. Once upon a time a young girl was put in here to get her away from a young man and he got into the barrel and turned himself round into the nunnery and there was great excitement.

I have for a wonder been on board all the day and evening but have not been lonesome for the vessel has been over run with company and callers. Everybody I ever met and some besides.

I had the accounts to settle up and father had the shore business to settle, and the clearing of his vessel. The room was crowded all the evening, but father went fast asleep and never woke up until they had all gone. I want to start for home, and I also hate to leave here. Everybody has been kindness itself, especially Mr. Rodilico, who has done everything in his power that I might have a good time. It is too bad I could not like him better, but I could not. There was not a friend he owned but what he used them for a good time for me and was lavish with fruit, flowers and wine. His last gift before the vessel left was a dozen bottles of Muscatel wine, which he knew I liked best of all. I cannot describe him to you, but when we arrived home the following letter had been received by my mother, and it is a fair sample of Mr. Rodilico on the whole:

TRAPINA, April li 21st, 1884.

Be not surprised if a unknown young man dares to address you for the first time.

The cordialness whereof Mr. Atwood honored me during his stay here[,] makes me believe possible you will grant me the ambition of becoming acquainted to his whole family.

Having been for some years in correspondence with Mr. Stewart,[G] I succeeded in loading the Charles Stewart, thence the occasion of spending more than a fortnight together with Mr. Atwood and Miss Hattie.

The habitual mildness of his temper soon won my affection and esteem, and I should be very much flattered if the same feelings were me allowed for the entire family.

I presume you worthy of Mr. Atwood's love. He remembered you in any occasion. Was he presented with some good wine? He warned his daughter to save it for her mother.

Was he in some beautiful garden? He wondered what you would have thought about. Everywhere and any time he thought of you. The first picture in the album–your own–was the best. What I wish for him is the chance of remaining home and to trade among the rest on salt, so I'll have the hope of his intercourse and lasting friendship.

Such are the human events. You may have had the frequence of acquaintances for years and years, but you perhaps don't feel for them the same you do for a friend just acquainted.

I pray you to excuse me my mistaken expression in this letter. I have very likely appeared ridiculous to Miss Hattie, speaking to her in a language which is not mine, but this time I do rely on Miss Bllandria's [Blandina's] bounty for my written English. If it is true, the latter has not the calm temper of her father, yet the openness of her figure, the artistic harmony of her features make me presume her soul full of courtesy for a stranger as I am, and if so I shall be infinately rewarded for the partiality I dared show for her picture. Was there no objection, could I write better in your language, I would pay my compliments to the good learned Miss Mary but I am fearful with her prepossessing smile she would laugh at my poor english.

Please give my love to the rest of your children and believe me with all respect.

MRS. HORACE ATWOOD

Hampden

your faithful servant

(signed)

NICOLO S. RODILICO

P.S. "Charles Stewart" left Trapani on the 17th inst I am sorry she had till now bad wind.

R

Now when I saw this letter it set me thinking. Mr. Rodilico was always looking at the album and admiring Blandina's picture, but he judged her wrong. She was always worse than I in seeing the ridiculous side of life and in showing it also, and one day he asked me the meaning of "prepossessed," so I suppose he was composing that letter while we were there.

But I cannot, nevertheless, forget all his kindness even if I could not accept it in a different spirit, I knew he meant well.

We are all on board the *Mercidita* to dinner. Such a funny cabin as she has. A large one, and following the shape of the stern was a couch all the way around, upholstered in red velvet. Father took a nap after dinner and Cap. Preston and I listened while Mr. Rodilico read out of an English book, and it nearly finished us both. It was on the months of the year, and told what our luck ought to be, birthstones, diseases and a lot of trash, and of all the questions that were asked. It was better than a poor play.

At three o'clock we all went ashore for the final good byes. After this, some of us came on board, but father went to market for the last time, and when he came back he had three Norwegian sea captains with him. All very pleasant.

I have enjoyed the Swedes and Norwegian acquaintances very much. They are nice people.

In the evening we all went to see "Boccacio"[G] played. It was very good, and then on board for the last time in Trapani, Sicily.

*'I landed
bird cage in hand
and said good bye.'*

Chapter Seventeen
HOMEWARD BOUND

April 17th. At sea today, bound for Rockland, Maine. Capt. Preston and Mr. Rodilico came on board for a last goodbye, and we put to sea. How still everything was! It was almost uncanny.

I had been living such a gay life that I was almost bewildered with the stillness. I watched Trapani disappear with sadness, for I had enjoyed every moment of our stay there. Before I left I was deluged with wine, flowers, fruit, oranges, lemons and plums. I bought gloves, umbrellas and wine for home.

Head winds must be proverbial in the Mediterranean Sea for we have had our share and all we can do is to wear ship, wear ship, walk the deck, walk the deck, and at last the Island of Sardinia is in sight. I have not overcome my desire to go into harbor there.

I sew and read and talk, which is my strongest achievement but after such an entertainment as the Italians gave us, and such a babel of voices, my efforts seem tame for when the Italians talk you would think they were mad. They shake themselves and their fists in each others faces, and you would surely think it a row, but they are only conversing.

A fair wind favors us after the calm and in a few hours it changes to a head wind and blows a gale. I was making some lemon pies and they all ran out into the oven, the vessel rolled so, but we have company in our misery, for there are three vessels in sight.

My pigeon is sitting and I hope for some little ones but one day we discovered that both pigeons were laying and I thought I was going to have lots of baby pigeons, and father said they would not hatch on account of their both being females.

That was the straw that broke the camel's back. I never knew that before.

I carried those pigeons home and they were so white and handsome, but I got so I let them out and they would go and wash in the sink drain and such looking things I never saw. Finally they died.

On April 26th my nineteenth birthday. I am in latitude 39 degrees, 22 minutes N., longitude 5 degrees, 11 minutes E. A year ago today I was in the Indian Ocean on my way to Australia. Head winds and rough seas today.

An Italian from Alicante,[G] Sicily, bound for

Charleston, South Carolina. We spoke him about four P. M. He asked: "What health there will be in Charleston?" Also, "Did we have any tobacco to spare?" We did not have any. Later on he signaled for our longitude by chronometer.

The only excitement was my kitten having a fit. I thought she was possessed of a devil. She ran up the sides of the cabin and held onto the blinds with a cry that would affect the strongest nerves. One day is enough of these per-fermances.

A fearful gale and such a short and choppy sea. It just picks the vessel up and drops her. We are under short sail and rolling something fearful.

Salt is a heavy cargo and the vessel is a dead weight for the seas to handle.

Father is very sick and had to go to bed with the pain in his side. After three hours I got it relieved with mustard poultices. I retired at nine but the vessel rolled so I got up at eleven, just to hold on.

Now we are off the coast of Algeria and almost into the harbor of Algeris [Algiers], and it is a queer looking place with a high wall around it. One of the most fascinating things on this trip is the different views of cities and towns on the coast.

As I awake and go on deck on May ninth, Gibraltar, Spain, and Cereta,[G] Africa are in plain sight; one looks like a giant, the other like a pigmy. We have a nice east wind and at nine o'clock are up to Gibraltar Rock, take a stray breeze and swift current and fairly race past towns, light houses and capes, and at twelve noon are once more in the Atlantic Ocean. We make fast time and are shortening the distance very fast. The usual life at sea. A dead whale excites us a little, and signaling vessels. Father's health is poor and it keeps me thinking what to do for him. On May twenty-eight we pass a small cake of ice. This is pretty far south to find signs of icebergs.

I go on deck and take command of the ship. Keep father and the mate laughing, and the sailor on a broad grin.

We pass a whaler and after dark can see the fire from its try works[G] where they were cutting in a whale. It looked like a lighthouse. I have to patch the black bunting dress, what will they say? I have only owned that dress a year and a half, and it was second-hand at that.

On June the eighth the air smells plainly of the shore. We pass a keg with a flag on it that has gotten away from some fisherman's lines. The next day is foggy and I have a new experience. We are near the shore and have not had a sight of the sun for two days. Sail is shortened as father hears a fog bell, how dismal it sounds! You cannot see ten feet away. How faint it dies out. It may be a fisherman anchored on a shoal. The vessel is hove to,[G] and sounding[G] taken, nothing at fifty fathoms. It is an uncanny feeling creeping along in a thick fog.

During the afternoon it looks like soundings, and once more the lead is "hove over" and we get soundings at forty fathoms, and find it on the chart. The sun peeps out, we rush for instruments, and time, and get "a sight" which puts us back from dead reckoning.[G]

The fog lifts and a brig is close at hand. I am tired out with excitement. Tell about "nothing doing at sea," try a voyage and see for yourself, you will never be sorry.

Sixty miles from Rockland,[G] Maine, and I watch for land, and see drift wood, lobster pots and something like a hoop skirt drift by. Mt. Desert in sight! The highest land on the Atlantic coast, and I sight the United States of America for the first time for eighteen months.

Mt. Desert Rock Lighthouse, Maine.
(Isleboro Museum, National Park Service)

Then we discover Mt. Desert Rock,[G] a small but very picturesque island. A light house on it and the sun shining on the white buildings make a very pretty picture. At three P. M. we pass the rock but the wind is dying out.

Wednesday, June 11, 1884. I got up at two A. M. and went on deck. We are three miles from Rockland, and the steamer from Boston to Bangor is in sight. The tide turns at six, and at ten we are in port. A boat comes out and tells us that Blaine[G] is nominated for President, which was the first news. Father goes ashore until four P. M. Just think of it only sixty miles from home! While he was gone, a boat with three young men in it came along side and brought me all the lobsters I could eat and give others. They were good.

At four, father comes on board and reports all well. Aunt Beckie[G] has a little girl named Kate Morey Cole. Willie Morey,[G] a cousin, married, but the best of all, a tug from home tomorrow bringing mother. I went to work with a vengence and got out the carpet, and it was about half down when three young ladies and two young men came on board. One of the young men was a Mr. Prescott who had taught at Hampden Academy[G] the fall before. After a pleasant call from them I finished up everything to be ready for tomorrow.

June 12th. I am up and about and excited. It is foggy but I keep my eye up the river. The fog lifts at twelve, I see a smoke stack up the river. At one, a tug is along side with her load of friends: Mother, Horace and Edward, my two brothers; Mrs. Whitmore, wife of the mate; Mr. Stewart,[G] the owner; Mrs. Vance,[G] his daughter; Walter Ross[G] of Bangor as captain.

The first words mother spoke to me were:

"You are not half as black as I thought you would be."

Didn't it seem good to see them all again and there were no idle moments. Such a chatter with eating and visiting.

While in Tasmania we got some roots and sticks for canes, and on the voyage I had sandpapered and shellaced and varnished them until they looked pretty nice, so I asked Mr. Stewart to accept one, and he was very much pleased and gave me a kiss for every joint there was in the cane, but I have forgotten now the number of joints. I know it made a great laugh at the time.

The tug stays down to take us over to Fox Island[G]

Waterfront, Hampden, Maine. (Hampden Historical Society)

tomorrow where the vessel is to unload.

After being towed to North Haven[G] mother and the boys are to stay down with father on the vessel also Mrs. Whitmore and I am to go home on the tug tonight.

After the Custom House officer had passed us, we loaded my trunk, wine and figs onto the tug, and saying good bye to the bark *Charles Stewart*, and my father whom I hated to leave yet glad to be at home again, we start for Hampden, Maine.

A delightful trip up the river, and at five P. M. the tug

whistled like mad for Hampden wharf, and we came along side with home in sight. Mr. Stewart[G] and Capt. Ross tried to make me cry, even offered to bring an onion, but I did not want to cry.

I landed bird cage in hand and said good bye. A team rushes down the hill and Mr. Delano,[G] the wharf agent, takes me and all my luggage up the hills so familiar and beautiful.

It is June and Academy Hill is beautiful in its new foliage.

The first one I see is my sister Annie, who is waiting for me. How she has grown. Blandina seems much older, Mary just the same. Left my trunk keys on the vessel, but we made some others fit.

There was not much to see. The yellow bed ticking dress, plum colored skirt and Japanese silk that had actually dropped apart, had been committed to the sea I loved so well. So ends this voyage a happy one.

EPILOGUE

It was again my good fortune to have the bark for my ocean home. On October twenty-first, 1884, I went on board again "bag and baggage" for another trip, this time to Sicily. Our Mr. Whitmore had become "Capt."Whitmore and commanded his own vessel. He was succeeded by a Hampden man, Mr. Ellis. We had the same old steward and a part of the old crew. Our voyage was uneventful, except that I got a scare from too close contact with a wicked looking waterspout. It barely missed us, but it makes one shudder to think what might have happened. On December 20th we arrived at Messina,^G after our letters had been pierced with a sharp knife and fumigated, and we had encountered much more "red tape," we went on shore. The beggars! I thought I had seen some before, but they did not compare with these. The crew celebrated Christmas by getting gloriously drunk. We were entertained royally by Mr. Paino. Strange to say I began my musical education in Italy, for it was at the home of this gentleman that I began my lessons on the piano under my teacher Antonio.

We saw much of a funny little fellow whom we called "One Boston." All the English at his command was "Lady, dear lady, me, one Boston go." Meaning he had been to Boston once. I received several letters from Mr. Rodilico.

On Feb. 5, 1885, we left Messina for home. That night we discovered that we had a stowaway on board, a Swiss, Charles Bieri,^G by name, who was a brother of one of the crew and an artist of no mean talent, as several paintings on the walls of my home today bear testimony.

A few days out, the bark caught fire in the galley but no damage was done.

On April 2d we were off the coast of Massachusetts, and at six P. M. a tug offered to take us in to Boston Harbor for fifty dollars. The offer was accepted, and at midnight we arrived at our berth. Our voyage was ended, likewise my career as a seawoman.

Possibly you will be interested to know the fate of the bark.

The first voyage after father gave her up, on her return from Scotland, she stuck on Rugged Island,[G] Penobscot Bay, and all that was saved was a few spars. It was a dense fog, and the fog bells were heard, but the captain[G] did not think it necessary to put to sea so she struck the rocks and went to the bottom. When father came home with the news I could not realize at first that it was so.

It is no exaggeration to say that it nearly broke my heart.

A life on the ocean wave,
A home on the rolling deep,
Where the scattered waters rave,
And the winds their revels keep!
Like an eagle caged, I pine
On this dull, unchanging shore;
Oh, give me the flashing brine,
The spray and the tempest roar!

Once more on the deck I stand
Of my own swift-gliding craft,
Set sail! farewell to the land,
The gale follows far abaft;

We shoot thro' the sparkling foam,
Like an ocean bird set free;
Like the ocean bird, our home
We'll find far out on the sea!

The land is no longer in view,
The clouds have begun to frown,
But with a stout vessel and crew,
We'll say let the storm come down!
And the song of our heart shall be,
While the winds and the waters rave,
A life on the heaving sea.
A home on the bounding wave!

                              –Old Song^G

THE END

Background and Notes

HATTIE ATWOOD

Imagine, if you can, a girl seventeen years and nine months old, five feet five inches high, weight one hundred pounds, dull expressionless blue eyes, brown hair painfully straight, large mouth, regular teeth, generous nose and ears, high cheek bones, loud full voice, unconquerable temper, and complexion (as her mother often told her) like a light-colored Indian, and it will not need a magnifying glass or encyclopedia to understand why I had never received those tender affections from the opposite sex [such as her two older sisters had received]. Nevertheless I was not a bad girl at heart and had many friends among my schoolmates.

This, as she humorously described herself two decades later, was the high-spirited girl who at the end of January, 1883, sailed from New York in the bark *Charles Stewart*, of which her father was master, went around the world, and in June, 1884, returned as a young lady of nineteen to Rockland, Maine, and to her home in nearby Hampden, Maine.

Hattie Atwood, the daughter of Captain Horace Atwood and his wife Harriet Morey Atwood, was born on April 26, 1865, in Hampden, a small port, mill, and farming town on the Penobscot five miles below Bangor. In 1860, according to census figures, the population was 3085; by 1880 it had declined to 2911. Its principal claim to fame was that it had been pillaged by the British in the War of 1812. The Atwood house stood on Main Street next to the still extant Hampden Academy building.[1] In the rear its large lot reached all the way down to the river. In this comfortable house she grew up with her three sisters Blandina, Mary Peru, and Annie, and her two brothers Horace Welcome and Edward M[orey?]. The two elder girls, Blandina (born 1862) and Mary Peru (born 1863), had come into the world at sea—Blandina, as her name indicates, on board Captain Atwood's then command, the ship *Blandina Dudley*; Mary Peru, as her name shows, off the coast of Peru.[2] Annie was born in 1869.

Though not born aboard a ship as her elder sisters were, Hattie started her maritime career extremely early. In 1868 as a toddler she sailed around the Horn to Valparaiso, Chile, with her father and mother in the *Garibaldi*, the ship of which Atwood then was master. As she says in her book, she spent her third birthday on the Pacific.[3] Later all the girls attended the District 3 school in Hampden. In 1873, for instance, Blandine [sic], Mary, Hattie, and Annie aged respectively 11, 10, 8, and 4 are listed as scholars.[4] Though the early records of the Hampden Academy are missing, it is almost certain that Hattie went on to it. Where else would she have learned to write with so much verve and color?

In 1883 when he was planning his voyage to Hobart and Brisbane Captain Atwood, according to Hattie, invited Blandina and Mary to accompany him. But they evidently had beaux and, as Hattie amusingly phrases it in a parody of the super-"delicate" language of the time, on learning how long the trip would be, "decided they could not be deprived so long of those tender affections that come to most young ladies of twenty and twenty-one years of age, thereupon they gave up the trip to remain near those affections." But Hattie, who wryly but with great good humor casts herself in the role of the ugly duckling, the poor Cinderella who had no such "tender affections" and had to wear all the cast-off clothes of her elder sisters, jumped at the chance to go with father to see the world. And see much of it she did. Furthermore, now out of the shadow of her sisters, she became a popular figure in the parties and sightseeing trips in which she, the daughters and wives of other captains, and young officers from other ships happily figured. She even acquired a Sicilian beau so enamored that early every day he brought her huge bouquets of flowers and wanted to marry—no, not Hattie, alas, but her sister Mary, with whose picture he had fallen in love!

—

Then came the years she chronicles so well in her book. She leaves Hampden January 12, 1883; she stays the night in Bangor with her aunt and uncle. On the 13th she takes the train to Boston, which she evidently had never previously visited. Staying there with her mother's sister Kate Morey, she spends three days sightseeing. Then she proceeds by the then-usual way to travel to New York: railroad from Boston to Fall River and Fall River Steamship Line boat from there to New York. There she is met by her father. On January 27th the *Charles Stewart* is cleared for departure.[5] On the 29th the bark is ready to sail. On the 30th[6] Hattie is at last off on her adventuresome trip around the world.[7] She does not return to the United States until June 11, 1884, when the *Charles Stewart* finally puts into Rockland harbor in Maine. The next day, in company with her mother and two brothers, who have come down to Rockland to meet her, she steams in the tug up the Penobscot to Hampden. She is home.

But, as the brief epilogue to her book explains, she has still not lost her zest for seafaring. Four months later, on October 21, she again sails with her father, this time on the much briefer voyage from Bangor to Messina, Sicily, and back. They arrive in Messina on December 20th. On February 5th, 1885, they leave for the United States, arriving in Boston on April 2nd, just two weeks before Hattie's 20th birthday.

———

On her return to Maine from her second voyage, Hattie's life at sea abruptly ends, and soon an entirely new and far less dramatic one begins. On September 24, 1886, she and Edgar A. Freeman of Norton, Massachuestts, register at the Hampden Town Hall their intention to marry, and on October 14th they are married in Boston by the Rev. S. H. Hayes, whom her father may well have met when Mr. Hayes was acting pastor of the Salem and Mariner's Church in that city. The couple seems to have gone immediately to live in Norton. Hattie was to live there until Edgar's death in 1924. One wonders why this vigorous young woman who had thoroughly enjoyed not only the excitement of seafaring but had learned navigation and at times appears to have navigated the bark,[8] kept her father's accounts and the bark's meteorological logs, even in tight places had taken the wheel of the vessel, who had delighted in seeing Tasmania, Queensland, Valparaiso, the guano islands, the Rock of Gibraltar, Barcelona, and the ancient cities of Sicily, who loved merry parties and flirting and meeting people, decided to tie herself down in a small Massachusetts town by marrying a man 23 years older.

Edgar Freeman had been born in West Bridgewater, a town near Norton, on February 23, 1842.[9] His mother Jerusha came from Norton and was a member of the prominent Lane family there. His father's Freeman family was an important one in Norton. Its members were as numerous in

Norton as the Atwoods were in Hampden and its surrounding towns. By 1850 the census records him, his mother, and his two brothers as living in the house of his uncle Henry Sanforth Freeman in Barrowsville, one of the several small hamlets that make up the town of Norton. Edgar was then 8 years old.

Twelve years later at the outbreak of the Civil War, Freeman enlisted on August 9, 1862, as a volunteer in Company H of the 40th Massachusetts Infantry Regiment. At that time he listed himself as a farmer. He was wounded a number of times, was frequently in the hospital, and lost the full use of one hand. A case of measles when in the army resulted in partial blindness in both eyes. He was mustered out on June 16, 1865, in Richmond, Virginia, at the rank of corporal and returned to Norton.

Two years later in 1867 he married Emily Jane Wheeler of Rehobeth, another small town close to Norton. Their first child Jessica, a daughter born in 1868, lived only a few months. In 1870 a son, Charles A. Freeman, was born, whom Hattie was to help bring up and in whose house in Connecticut she would live for sixteen years after Edgar's death. In the census of that year Edgar again listed himself as a farmer. In 1874, evidently tired of living with her husband's relatives, Emily, out of her own or her family's money, bought for herself and Edgar from the Lanes a house on a three-acre lot in the center of Barrowsville. The deed was in Emily's name; Edgar was given only a life interest in the property. In 1880 Emily, Edgar, and Charles were still living in Barrowsville, together with Emily's grandmother Wealthy Horr. Emily died, aged 34, of pneumonia on February 16, 1881.

When five years later, on October 14, 1886, Edgar married Hattie, she was 21, he 44, and Charles 16. Hattie was much closer in age to her stepson Charles than to her bridegroom. According to an application for a veteran's disability pension he later made, Edgar was 5 feet, 4 3/4 inches in height, with a light complexion and brown hair.

How Hattie, living in a small seaport town in Maine, happened to meet and marry this undistinguished middle-aged veteran and widower in an equally small town in far-off southern Massachusetts is unclear. There were Moreys (Hattie's mother's maiden name) and Freemans in both Hampden and Norton.[10] Possibly there was some family tie. There is a more probable, though by no means certain, explanation of the mystery suggested by Jennie F. Copeland's account in her book *Every Day but Sunday*[11] of the straw-hat industry that flourished in mid-nineteenth-century Norton, and more particularly in Mansfield, a larger, more industrialized town bordering Norton to the north. Making straw hats began in the area as a cottage craft, but by the middle 1880s factories had developed that required large numbers of women workers. Many of the young women who were recruited came from farms or small towns in Maine. The work was seasonal. They could come to Mansfield in the late fall after the rye straw of which the hats were made had been harvested and dried, board in local homes, earn good money over the winter when they were not needed on their farms in Maine, and in the early spring return to Maine with a respectable sum to spend or put away toward marriage. But Mansfield was not all work. They had time for parties, dances, organized sightseeing trips to Boston and elsewhere, and other social—or indeed romantic —activities that made their stay in Mansfield fun as well as profitable. Many of them never did return to Maine, but stayed to marry men from Mansfield and its surrounding towns. The straw-hat mills, Copeland says, acted as informal but very successful "matrimonial bureaus." It is therefore possible, perhaps even probable, that Hattie, bored with life in Hampden after her exciting years of voyaging around the world and wanting to earn a little cash money—or even find a husband?—came to Mansfield, met Edgar Freeman at work or at some festivity, and decided to marry him.

Whatever beginning there was, for the 38 years from her marriage until Edgar's death Hattie lived in Norton, evidently contentedly, as a housewife and loving stepmother. Because of his disability from his war service, Edgar applied for and received as time went by higher and higher veteran's pensions. But despite this increasing income Hattie and Edgar were far from well off. In 1894 he was working as a teamster for the local factory that manufactured boxes for the jewelry industry of adjoining Attleboro. In a Norton valuation book of 1899 Hattie and he were listed as owning no real estate, and according to the census of 1900 they lived in a rented house—perhaps mill housing—on West Main Street near the factory where Edgar loaded his wagon. In 1902, however, they were prospering enough to buy for $1350 a house of their own on Main Street. This house they occupied until Edgar died, except for the years 1906 to 1910.

For in 1905 Edgar was appointed superintendent of the Almshouse and Town [Poor] Farm at a salary of $300 a year. Hattie and he lived at the Almshouse from 1906 until it was closed in 1910. It was in 1907, when she was living there, that she revised her diary or journal of her youthful voyages into the book *A Trip Around the World* and had it privately printed in Bangor, Maine, near her birthplace.[12]

Why did she edit and print it at this time? She says

Edgar Freeman, in old age. (Author's Collection)

it was partly to please her father who, getting on in years (he was then 78 and would die in 1910), would enjoy reviving memories of the voyage they had made so long before. But one wonders whether Hattie had found her girlhood diary on her mother's death the previous year. She almost surely went back to Hampden to the funeral and to look over what belongings of hers remained in the old homestead. Or did she inherit from her mother a little money that she could use to pay for the printing? It may be significant that also in 1907 Hattie and Edgar paid off the mortgage on their house, though by 1910 they had taken out another one. Or it may simply be that as wife of the superintendent of the Almshouse she had domestic help from pauper inmates and thus leisure to prepare her wonderful little book for publication.

By 1914 Hattie and Edgar owned not only their own house on Main Street but also two other adjoining tracts of land, six acres altogether.

On November 9, 1924, Edgar was struck by an automobile while crossing Main Street near his home and died in Sturdy Memorial Hospital in Attleboro of fracture of the skull. He was 82 years old. Hattie was 59.

—

So once again came a drastic change in Hattie's life. She was appointed administrix of Edgar's estate and sold much if not all of their property in Norton. Then she moved to the house of her stepson Charles Freeman, with whom over the years she must have developed an unusually warm relationship, at 117 West Broad Street, Pawcatuck, Connecticut, really an over-the-border suburb of Westerly, Rhode Island.[13] There she lived for the rest of her life except for a few months in a nursing home just before her death. As one can imagine, Hattie still being Hattie, it was not a dull life she led. Living in the downstairs apartment in her stepson's house, she was close to his children and later his grandchildren. She was a marvelous story-teller and delighted in entertaining them with tales of her overseas adventures. She enjoyed playing games with them. She liked whist and pinochle and cribbage and crossword puzzles. She gave lectures to organizations in her church. She was long active in the women's branch of the G.A.R. and liked to parade with the veterans on Memorial Day.[14] During World War I she belonged to the Women's Relief Corps in Attleboro. She kept close ties with Maine and with her many friends and relations in Norton and often visited there. She reinspired her love of traveling, visiting her sisters and brothers and nieces and nephews all over the United States from Maine to Minnesota to California. She traveled to Alaska. She lived for a time in Florida. She loved to talk (as she tells us in her book). All her life she seems to have been the same vital, active, friendly, outgoing person she had been on that memorable trip around the world so long ago.

For such a vibrant and vigorous woman her end was sad. Although in 1936 she had happily traveled out to Minnesota to visit her niece Henrietta Atwood Briggs, by 1938 she had failed so much that she had to be moved from the house in Pawcatuck to a nursing home in Westerly, Rhode Island. When Mrs. Briggs visited her there, she was only the pitiful shell of herself, shrunken, weeping, despondent. She died in the nursing home on October 27, 1939, at the age of 74. She was buried with her husband Edgar, his first wife Emily, and their baby Jessica in the Common Cemetery in Norton. Her stepson Charles (died 1961) and his wife Bertha Valentine lie nearby.

CAPTAIN HORACE ATWOOD

Hattie's father Horace Atwood, master of the bark *Charles Stewart* on both voyages taken by Hattie, was not unlike his daughter. "He was," said a Hampden man who had known him well, always a notable figure. "Tall in stature and large in frame, with his genial presence he added interest to any gathering. Possessing a wealth of humor and abounding in good nature he was always a welcome visitor."[15] In her book Hattie, too, testifies to his commanding size, describing him as six feet tall and weighing 250 pounds. He was born in Hampden, the son of William and Ruth Atwood of Hampden, on January 2, 1829. The Atwoods were a sea-

Captain Horace Atwood (from the original book)

going family. According to one report,[16] five of Horace's uncles, sons of Jesse Atwood, were lost at sea. Horace's cousin George Atwood of Bangor was an active sea captain during the same years that Horace was. Other Atwood ship-masters also appear in the maritime records of the Hampden-Bangor region. When no first name or initial is given, it is difficult to ascertain which Atwood is meant.

Horace Atwood was a mariner or associated with ships all his life, even though the 1850 Hampden census listed him as a farmer, probably working on his father's farm, as many Maine men who went to sea were employed when not afloat.[17] But in the same year he was master of the schooner on which William Morey, Jr., his future wife's 13-year-old brother, made his first voyage.[18] It was probably sometime between 1852 and 1855 that he was mate of the famous clipper ship *Gem of the Ocean,*[v] launched in Medford, Massachusetts, in 1852. *Gem* was a celebrated vessel that on one of her voyages set a speed record by running from Canton, China, to New York in 89 days.[19] In October of 1856 Horace Atwood sailed from Charlestown, Massachusetts, as the first master of the new ship *Blandina Dudley*[v], which was employed in trades to the East Indies. Her maiden voyage was to Calcutta, which she reached in March, 1857.[20] He was to hold that command through 1863.

On August 13, 1857, he was married in Boston by the Rev. S. Strater to Harriet Morey, aged 25, eldest of the ten children of William Morey and Mary Morey of Hampden. Horace was 28. The marriage record lists him as "master mariner of Boston." Soon enough, probably within a year, Harriet too might well have called herself a "mariner": for a number of years she accompanied Horace on his voyages. As already noted, her first two daughters were born at sea, and Hattie records in her book that her own third birthday (in 1868) was spent with her mother and father on the Pacific and that she visited Valparaiso with them.

That 1868 voyage was in Horace's next command, the *Garibaldi*[v] of Newburyport,[21] a prominent vessel in the California grain fleet, which annually carried on a triangular trade from New York to San Francisco and on to Liverpool. The ships sailed, often in ballast[G] or with a few trade goods, around the Horn to California, where they loaded large cargoes of the wheat and other grain being grown there. Some of granite paving stones they brought to San Francisco as ballast are still in place.[22] Then they carried the shipload of grain to Liverpool, where it could be sold at great profit. Thence they returned across the Atlantic to New York loaded with British manufactured goods. The *Garibaldi* also made several voyages to the East, passages to which Atwood had already become accustomed in the *Blandina Dudley*.

In 1869 he bought for $3000 from his cousin James A. Swett of Hampden the Swett house and 18-acre farm in Hampden, lying between Main Street and the Penobscot River and encompassing much of what is now the center of the village of Hampden.[23] The farm as bought by Benjamin Swett in 1793 had originally extended a mile inland from the shore, had included the present sites of the Hampden Town Hall and Hampden Academy, and 1000 feet of shore frontage including Squaw and Samoset Points. The house on the property may have been the original Swett farmhouse. This was to be home to the Atwoods until Horace's death in 1911. In it Hattie and her sisters and brothers grew up. Parts of the farm were still in the possession of the Atwood children until 1919. Now a landowner, Horace was appointed Hampden School Agent, a post he held until 1879.

By 1871 he was master of the *Tennyson*[V] of Newburyport, which was, like the *Blandina Dudley* and the *Garibaldi*, in the East India trade. She was also in the ice trade, of which more below.

In the following year (1872) Atwood took what must surely have been the most dangerous and exciting voyage of his life. He was then the master of the *Montana*[V], one of Tudor and Company's famous ships that carried ice cut from New England ponds to Calcutta, Rangoon, and other ports.[24] Though the trade was highly profitable, it was also dangerous. The ice was packed to prevent melting in hay or sawdust. If the hay or sawdust got wet it tended by spontaneous combustion to burst into flame, very frequently setting on fire the vessel which was carrying it. Many ice ships were lost to such fires. The *Montana*, bound for Rangoon, had rounded the Cape of Good Hope and was in the middle of the Indian Ocean nearly a thousand miles from any land when fire was discovered in the forepeak[G]. No amount of dousing it with sea water could put it out. Atwood set a course for the nearest land, St. Paul Island[G], a barren, uninhabited rock in the very middle of the Indian Ocean. The vessel, with fire eating at her vitals, became hotter and hotter until the crew often were taking to the rigging to escape the flames that belched out through the deck seams. Finally in a roaring gale the *Montana* reached St. Paul and let go her anchor. By good fortune the anchor held. What provisions and water that could be gathered were put in the boats and ferried to shore. Soon the ship "erupted" and sank:

The crew had not been on shore many hours when, with a frightful roar, the flames burst through the ship's decks and soared aloft in a red and black torrent, eating up the sails and rigging like chaff. Soon the masts fell, and before night there was nothing left of the ship but her hull under water and a blackened heap of ice in its depths.[25]

Then, to add to the drama, the island itself, which was the remainder of a volcanic cone, began to show signs of erupting and was shaken by a violent earthquake. For some time the men, fearful that the island would blow up, lived largely on the abundant mussels and fish for which the island was well-known. Although St. Paul was rarely visited, a large British ship finally loomed up out a dense fog. Atwood and his crew were appalled to see that, not knowing her danger, she was steering straight for the rocks. They made what noise they could, and at the last possible moment the crew aboard the ship standing into danger heard their warnings and sheered off. The Americans were taken aboard and transported to Rangoon. Atwood returned home through the Suez Canal in a steamer.

As far as can be ascertained, Horace Atwood's next command was the ship *Victoria*[V], again a Newburyport vessel. An article published in the *Bangor Daily Commercial* in 1926 reports that he remained her master for a number of years, and with him in command her "flag floated over the waters of about every maritime country on the globe with the exception of China." He may have assumed command in 1873, the year the *Victoria* was launched. He was certainly her master from 1874 to 1878, the year in which the ship—evidently mistakenly—was reported as lost.[27] Probably it was in her that in 1878 Atwood took along his little 12-year-old son Horace Welcome Atwood to Liverpool as cabin boy.

What Atwood was doing from 1879 to 1881 is uncertain. Perhaps he was ashore farming; perhaps he had another command. But, as the title of Hattie's book indicates, from 1883 to April, 1885, he was master of the bark *Charles Stewart,* owned in Bangor, Maine, but technically sailing out of New York. His first voyage with Hattie was also his first as master of his new command. With her he sailed, as has already been said, on January 29, 1883, from New York for Hobart, Tasmania—the voyage she recounts in her book —returning to Rockland, Maine, in June, 1884. A month later in July, 1884, without Hattie he took the bark from Bangor, Maine, to Scotland, returning to Bangor on October 4 with a cargo of coal. In the same month, again with Hattie as his shipmate, he left Bangor October 21, 1884, returning to Boston on April 2, 1885. This was his last ocean voyage. On May 21 a new Certificate of Registration[28] for the *Charles Stewart* substituted the name of Johnson Grant for his as master. His career as a sea captain was over.

Why he retired is clear. In April, 1885, he was 56 years old. He had been at sea for at least 35 years. His health was not good: in her book Hattie again and again notes that he is seriously ill and at times in pain. And—perhaps the most important and certainly the most historically interesting reason—he sees that the age of sail is drawing to a close. American sailing ships in deepwater trades are becoming scarce and, worse, unprofitable. Even little barks like the *Charles Stewart*, surviving in the tramping trades in the final decades of the nineteenth century, are becoming marginal. They cannot compete with the speed and reliability of the steamers. Writing at the end (September 11, 1884) in the Meteorological Log that he kept on his 1884 voyage on the *Charles Stewart* to Scotland Horace sadly notes : ". . . a very lonesome journey. Freights dull for all parts of the world. Too many steamers and sailing vessels for the work to do." Later, Hattie herself, writing on October 30, 1884 in the Meteorological Log she kept on her 1883-84 voyage to Messina, remarked that, "We see two steamers now to one sailing ship. It won't be long till sailing ships will be one of the passed and at present not of much account as they do not pay their running expenses." In her entry for November 25, 1883, writing of the vessels waiting near Cape Spartel to pass through the Straits of Gilbraltar, she struck much the same note, though emphasizing particularly the decline of the American merchant marine:

Out of the whole fleet here, we are the only American. How things have changed. Six large steam frigates turned [?] out from the Straits and two four masters. Grand sight and England's glory makes a Yank feel mean when compared with the American.

It was no wonder Atwood thought it time to quit.

But even though Horace Atwood was done with life at sea, he was not done with shipping and ships. On July 20 the following article appeared in the *Bangor Whig and Courier*: The steamer *Isma* is now commanded by Captain Horace Atwood. It is doing a splendid business, surprising even the owners. On hot afternoons many people go down river on the boat to catch the cool breezes. The *Isma* is a very pleasant boat on which to make an excursion.

Under "Special Notices" the following schedule was advertised:

Steamer ISMA
CAPT. HORACE ATWOOD

Will leave Ferry Slip every day at 6:30, 8:00,
and 11:00 A.M. and 2:30 and 4:30 P.M. touching at all
convenient landings on the river when signalled as
far as the Union Ice House and running to Hampden
on 8:00 and 11:00 A.M. and 2:30 P.M. trips.

A new picnic grove has been fitted up
expressly for the patrons of this steamer
at Squaw Point, Hampden.

RETURNING.
will leave Hampden at 9:00 A.M. and 1:00 and
5:40 P.M. and Union Ice House at 7:15 and 9:15 A.M.
and 1:15, 3:15, and 6:00 P.M.

Steamer Isma can be chartered for evening and
Sunday excursions by applying to
F. H. CLERGUE, President or
C. H. FIELD, Treasurer
Office at Bacon, Robinson and Co.'s [Coal?] Station

Horace Atwood was embarking on a new chapter in his life. He who had braved the storms and dangers of the seven seas was now captain of a small passenger and excursion steamer running between Bangor and Hampden. He had also developed Squaw Point, part of the large farm he had acquired twenty-five years before, into a picnic ground, a highly popular kind of resort in the 1880s. According to the previously cited article "Pleasant Session Held at Squaw Point" in the August 20, 1920, *Bangor Daily Commercial*, Squaw Point on the Penobscot River at Hampden was "one of nature's beauty spots" and had been frequented within living memory by the Squaw Indians. Even when he had bought it more than 25 years before he had been aware of "the resort possibilities of the picturesque locality." When he had retired from the sea and was not "engaged in farming or other avocations," the article goes on, by laying out paths and making rustic seats and bridges he had created a wonderful natural park, built a pavilion, and run the little steamer *Isma* to bring picnic parties to his grove as well as to transport regular passengers.

How long Atwood captained this steamer and how long the picnic grove lasted are unclear. When on October 8, 1886, the *Isma* is again advertised in the *Whig and Courier,* she is under new management, and Atwood is not mentioned. But those facts do not necessarily mean he was no longer in command. And on fresh water as well as on salt he could act the hero. At one time during his river career he even received a silver pitcher with his initials engraved on it for rescuing a boy who fell overboard, probably from the *Isma*.[29]

Then in 1893 still another chapter of his life began. On June 24 of that year the *Bath Enterprise* announced that

Captain Atwood had been "nominated to succeed Captain Flowers" as one of the two members of the Maine Board of Steamboat Inspectors.[30] His responsibility was to examine the hulls of passenger steamers operating in the state's inland waters. On June 29 he was sworn in for a full five-year term. His salary of $5.00 a day plus expenses was to be paid out of the inspection fees he collected. In 1898 he was appointed to a second five-year term.[31] But in 1903, tired of the extensive travel his duties demanded and feeling the effects of age, he evidently did not seek another term. He was then 74 years old.

His last years were spent in Hampden and in visiting his children, who had scattered all over the country. His wife Harriet—Hattie's mother—died in 1906. Horace himself died, aged 81, in Philadelphia in January of 1910 on a visit to one of his children.[32]

THE BARK *CHARLES STEWART*

The bark *Charles Stewart*, in which Hattie Atwood took both of her voyages, was named after the son of the vessel's principal owner Thomas Jefferson Stewart and himself a partner in T. J. Stewart and Company. Commissioned by T. J. Stewart, she was constructed in Belfast, Maine, in the well-known shipbuilding yards of George Washington Cotterill. She was launched on November 9, 1877. According to her first Certificate of Registration, signed November 6, 1877, her gross tonnage —large for a bark—was 629.9, her net 603. Her length was 143.4 feet, her breadth 33.3 feet, and her depth 18.3 feet. She had two decks and three masts, a billethead[G] (instead of a figurehead) at her bow and an elliptic stern. The poop[G] and the deck house[G] could be used for cargo. The galley was in the forward house. Her listings in *the Annual List of*

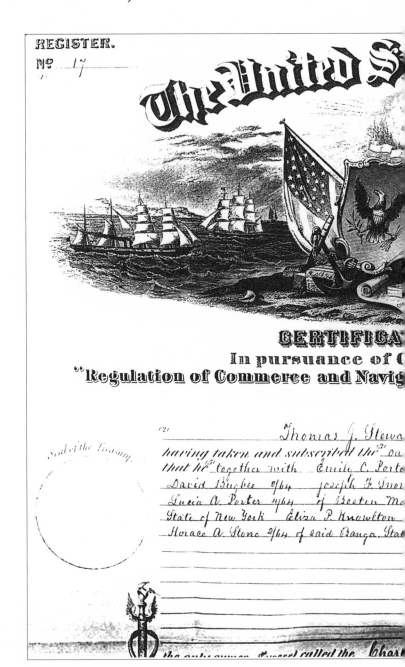

REGISTER.

Nº 17

The United S

CERTIFICA

In pursuance of (

"Regulation of Commerce and Navig

Seal of the Treasury.

(2)   Thomas J. Stewa

having taken and subscribed the[s] oa

that he[s] together with Emily C. Porte

David Bugbee ⁹/₆₄   Joseph F. Snor

Lucia A. Porter ⁴/₆₄ of Boston Ma

State of New York Eliza P. Knowlton

Horace A. Stone ²/₆₄ of said Bango. Stat

the only owner of vessel called the Char

Certificate of Registry for the bark 'Charles Stewart'

es of America

F REGISTRY,
er one, Title XLVIII,
," Revised Statutes of the United States,

of Bangor State of Maine

_____ required by law, and having [t] sworn _____

Mary M. Stewart 2/64 Mary A. Johnson 2/64 George A. Stone 2/64

of said Bangor David W. Pierce 2/64 of Orrington State aforesaid

trude C. Howe 2/64 of Brooklyn B. G. Neff 2/64 of New York

Stowe Vt Rosaline P. Vance 2/64 of Indianapolis and

are

of [t] New York

Merchant Vessels of the United States indicate that she was constructed of hackmatack (juniper), oak, and yellow pine with copper and iron fastenings. Her official number 125,623 was painted on her stern in white letters on a black ground.[33] The official identification letters[G] flown on her signal flag were J.S.Q.R. Throughout her whole service her home port was listed as New York. This was merely technical, meaning that the agents who handled the bark's business were in New York. Actually she was always owned by T. J. Stewart & Company in Bangor, Maine. Her last register (May, 1886) indicates that her stern had been changed from elliptic to square. She was rigged as a bark, square sails on foremast and mainmast, fore-and-aft on the mizzen.

The bark's first master was H. R. Powers of Orrington, Maine, just across the Penobscot River from Hampden. He continued in command from the bark's launching on November 7, 1877, until Horace Atwood took over in late 1882.[34] Atwood remained master until some time between April 2, 1885, when the *Charles Stewart* with Hattie aboard reached Boston harbor, and May 21, 1885, when a new Certificate of Enrolment was issued at Bangor listing Johnson Grant as master. It was Grant who was responsible for the vessel's loss.

For on the morning of September 17, 1886, on her return from a voyage to Greenock with coal—a repeat of the same trip Horace Atwood had made with his son Horace in 1884—the bark went ashore on reefs off the south side of Ragged Island, a small rocky islet just south of Matinicus in the very outermost part of Penobscot Bay.[35] According to Hattie,

. . . *it was a dense fog, and the fog bells were heard, but the captain [Johnson Grant] did not think it necessary to put to sea so she struck on the rocks and went to the bottom."*

The end of the vessel, however, was not so swift as Hattie makes it sound. The bark died slowly. Even though the *Bangor Daily Whig and Courier,* in a dispatch from Rockland, reported her "a total loss," an article on the following day (September 21) in the same paper was more hopeful:

THE CHARLES STEWART. The bark Charles Stewart, *which ran ashore on Ragged Island off Matinicus, Saturday morning, had not broken up when she was last heard from yesterday noon but was in good condition. It is not probable that she can be saved, however, as she has 700 tons of coal aboard and lies in a very bad condition. The coal was for the Maine Central [Railroad] but they [i.e., the railroad] lose nothing as it was to be delivered. There was no insurance on the vessel or on cargo. The* Charles Stewart *was a splendid vessel of 630 tons, built in Belfast in 1877, and had made numerous foreign voyages. Her owners were T.J. Stewart & Co., of this city, with parties in Belfast and New York.*

On September 24 the report was that "The tug *Ralph Ross*[36] came up yesterday from Ragged Island where the bark *Charles Stewart* is ashore. Nothing can be saved from the vessel but some rigging and a few chains, and it is difficult to secure these as the vessel is partly under water." Yet four days later the news was much more hopeful. In a dispatch from Rockland dated September 27, printed on the 28th, the paper said that "the bark has not strained much and it is hoped they can get her off." In order to lighten her to facilitate getting her off "the cargo of coal has been given to the inhabitants of Matinicus and they are taking it off." Free coal for the taking! Even on the 30th the Belfast *Republican Journal* held out hope that she could eventually be got off. But a storm in the middle of October finally destroyed her: "The *Charles Stewart* has gone to pieces," the *Journal* reported on October 14. "The wrecking crew was unable to do anything toward saving her." So at last the sad end came to the vessel Hattie so much loved. As she ends her own grieving farewell, "all that was saved was a few spars."

THE OWNERS

Throughout the whole life of the *Charles Stewart* her principal owner was Captain Thomas Jefferson Stewart (1823-90) of Bangor. It was he who commissioned her building in Belfast in 1877. His name is on the vessel's first Certificate of Registration. Some account of him, his sons, and his various business enterprises can explain a number of aspects of the two voyages that Hattie Atwood records in her book.[37]

Stewart began in the grocery business, but because of poor health went to sea and rose to be a master mariner. After his marriage in 1851 he returned to the grocery and provisioning business, both wholesale and retail, but also became a ship broker and maritime commission merchant.

The latter enterprises became so important that he sold the grocery business to his clerks so that he could concentrate on it. He soon became a major figure in Bangor commerce. He was a director of a number of the city's important banks. He founded, one imagines partly for his own use, several marine insurance companies. He was Portuguese consul to Maine and one of the port wardens. Of Thomas's four sons, Charles, Edward, Harry, and Rowland,[38] all except Harry became partners in the firm of T. J. Stewart & Company. Harry, the third son, went into the wholesale ice business and the manufacture of lumber and box shooks[39]—both enterprises meshing perfectly with the family firm's trade.

Charles Stewart (1854-1925), the eldest son for whom the bark was named, after traveling to various parts of Europe in his father's vessels, clerked in the company's office until 1875. He then became a partner with his uncle in a marine produce commission firm in New York City, but eventually returned to Bangor to become a partner with his brother Edward and his father. Later Rowland, the youngest son, also joined the firm but eventually left it to go into business on his own. After their father's death on March 6, 1890, Charles and Edward carried on T. J. Stewart & Company, with Charles as treasurer and general manager. It continued in altered form into the early twentieth century.

A great part of T. J. Stewart's success can be traced back to his innovative idea of carrying orange and lemon box shooks (the parts of a wooden box before it is put together), manufactured from Maine's abundant timber, to the fruit-growing regions of Spain, mainland Italy, and Sicily, where just such boxes were needed for exporting fruit to the United States. Thus Stewart's vessels were kept profitably loaded both going to and coming back from Europe. The firm's varied trade is clearly summed up in the obituary of Charles cited below:

> For many years the firm of T. J. Stewart & Sons carried on an extensive export trade in fruit box shooks, spoolwood and various kinds of long lumber, sending as many as 3,000,000 orange and lemon boxes yearly to Palermo, Messina and Augusta in the island of Sicily, and to Sorrento, Castellamare, Genoa and

Italian salt bark unloading salt at Vinalhaven.
(Vinalhaven Historical Society)

Leghorn in Italy; spoolwood[G] and deals[G] to ports in the United Kingdom and pine shipping boards to various ports in the West Indies, while during the height of the ice trade on the Penobscot they shipped many thousands of tons of that commodity to ports all along the Atlantic coast of the United States. The firm owned at the height of Bangor's prosperity as a seaport a fleet of square-rigged vessels, including the bark Thomas J. [error for Charles] Stewart, *which was lost on Ragged Island on the homeward voyage from Glasgow, and the brigs* Harry Stewart, Rabboni, Havilah *and* Mary Stewart, *the last named afterward rigged as a schooner; also the schooner* Edward Stewart.*

The greater part of the shook trade was carried on in Italian vessels, among which were the pretty barkentine Teresa Lovico, *the barks* Andrea Lovico, Emilia Ciampi, Ciampi Emilia, Michele, Vega, Ciarina *and the brig* Fortunata.[40] *Among the American vessels engaged in the trade were the Bangor brigs* Harry*

Smith, Fidelia, Rabboni, Havilah, Rachel Coney and Telos, and the bark T. J. [Charles?] Stewart. *In the days of the deal and spoolwood trade the Stewart firm chartered many British cargo steamers. . . . Many of the Italian shook carriers brought salt here or to Bucksport from Trapani and Augusta, Sicily, and from Cadiz in Spain, while the Americans on their homeward voyages usually brought salt from Turk's Islands [in the West Indies], Bonaire or Curacao [islands off the coast of Venezuela].*

With the death of the elder Stewart and the decline of the export trade, the firm gradually went out of business.

At the height of the trade more than four million box shooks were exported from Bangor in a single year, representing a value of $200,000. A major portion of the business was the passage back to the U.S. with salt both from Sicilian and other Mediterranean salt works and also from the West Indies. The salt, of course, was in great demand by the Maine fisheries. To the West Indies he exported in return Maine pine boards and other lumber. The Stewarts also imported coal, some from the Scottish mines and from the coal-exporting ports of the American South, delivering it to Boston, Bangor, and other New England ports.

The advertisement here, in the 1885 *Bangor and Brewer Directory*, provides a helpful summary of the business for which the *Charles Stewart* was built and sailed.

But though T. J. Stewart held the controlling interest in the *Charles Stewart* throughout her whole career, it should not be thought that he or even he and his sons were the sole owners. Just as when a whaling ship went out on a cruise a considerable number of persons (including the members of the crew) had "lays" or shares in her profits, so

T. J. STEWART & CO.,
Commission Merchants & Ship Brokers,

Lumber, Orange, Lemon, Raisin and Onion BOX SHOOKS FOR
EXPORT, Cement Barrel Heads and Staves, Spool Timber,
Etc. Shooks for Oil Cases, Fish, Cranberry
and other Boxes.

ICE PACKED FOR ANY VOYAGE A SPECIALTY.

Importers of Turks Island Salt by the Cargo,— same delivered to
any port in United States to order.

EXCELSIOR (Coarse and Fine).

Exchange St., cor. Washington,   Bangor, Maine.

Advertisement in the Bangor and Brewer Directory.

the owners of shares in the *Charles Stewart* included a number of small investors. The shares were phrased in sixty-fourths of the total ownership. Many of the minor shareholders were, as was usual at the time, relatives or friends of the Stewarts. As the years went by, some shareholders relinquished their shares and others took their places. Usually the captain had at least one share. Captain Powers, Horace Atwood's predecessor as master of the bark, owned two—or 1/32nd—as did Atwood's successor Johnson Grant, but Atwood for some unknown reason never owned any.

Here are the names and numbers of shares or fractions (sixty-fourths) of the owners of the *Charles Stewart* as listed in the registration certificate issued in New York on November 6, 1882, the first certificate that named Horace Atwood as the bark's master and the one that was operative during both of Hattie's voyages:

Barzillai G. Neff of New York City and State 2/64

[probably the bark's New York agent]

Charles M. Stewart of New York 2/64

Thomas J. Stewart 33/64

George A. Stone 1/32

Emily O. Porter 4/64 [Porter was the maiden name of T. J. Stewart's mother-in-law and occurs often as a middle name in the Stewart family]

Mary M. Stewart 2/64 [T. J.'s wife]

Joseph F. Snow 1/64

David Bugbee 2/64

Horace A. Stone 2/64

Mary A. Johnson 2/64 of Bangor, Maine

Eliza P. Knowlton 2/64 of Stowe, Vermont

Lucia S. Porter 4/64 of Boston, Massachusetts

Rosaline S. Vance 2/64 of Indianapolis, Indiana [T. J.'s daughter]

David W. Pierce 4/64 of Orrington, Maine

Note that T. J. Stewart keeps for himself a controlling interest, though only a thin majority of one (33 out of 64), of the shares. Hattie, unfortunately, had none.

CARGO

What, then, were the cargoes that the *Charles Stewart* carried during the years Horace Atwood was her master—and especially on the voyages on which Hattie sailed? The vessel was, as Hattie indicates by her title, a "merchantman bark" carrying cargoes hither and thither, either to sell them on her own account for the benefit of her owners or commissioned by third parties to transport goods from one part of the world to another. From the information about the Stewart firm's interests, especially from the 1885 advertisement quoted above; from what Hattie herself says in her book; and from the information given by the meteorological journals, it is not difficult to ascertain or at least surmise what the bark was carrying on each of Hattie's voyages.

By far the most interesting and varied cargoes were those on the 1883-84 voyage which eventually went all around the world. On this voyage the bark was not merely, as on the others, moving between two ports to transport cargo arranged for long in advance. Here, on the contrary, she was more of a "tramp" merchant vessel seeking cargo wherever her agents could find it for her, and indeed at times not knowing exactly where she would be going next until she reached port and found instructions from her agents or owners.

Thus on the first leg of this the longest of her voyages—the leg from New York to Hobart, Tasmania, and Brisbane, Australia—she carried all kinds of goods, from building materials to oysters. Whether the items were ordered by specific consignees or merely sent by T. J. Stewart on speculation is not clear. In either case the company had an agent in each port to receive them. Here is the list of the items on *Charles Stewart* consigned to or sold at Hobart as it appeared in the shipping news of the *Hobart Mercury* of May 12, 1883.[41] Note the reference to Hattie.

ARRIVED.–May 11.
Charles Stewart, American barque, 603 tons, Captain Horace Atwood, from New York 29th January, for Brisbane via Hobart. Passenger Cabin: Miss Atwood. Agents Macfarlane Bros. and Co.

IMPORTS.–May 11.
Charles Stewart, American barque, from New York.– 10 bls white duck, 51 css [cases] handles, 4,000 cc kerosene oil, 25,120 pcs [pieces] roofing slate, 30 css axes, 20 css oysters, 650 doors, 18 css whiting, 10 css milk, 200 kgs, 4 css nails, 105 pkgs woodenware, 9 cls

[coils?] rope, 50 bls resin, 40 css turpentine, 5 css agricultural implements, 6 css organs, 16 css clocks, 21 pkgs blacking, 3 css leather, 2 css hardware, 60 bxs [boxes] 20 qr-trcs [quarter-?] tobacco, 1 cs hay-knives, 2 bxs machinery, 12 css chairs, 2,423 pcs shelving, 2 css shovels, 2 bdls mop handles, and 37 css merchandise.

The list of the bark's imports into Brisbane as reported by the *Brisbane Courier* for Thursday, June 14, 1883[43] was much longer. Here it is:

ENTERED INWARDS

June 13.–*Charles Stewart*, American barque, 603 tons, Captain Horace Atwood, from New York via Hobart, with a general cargo. Webster and Co., agents.

IMPORTS

(A special charge is made on consignees' announcements inserted in this column.)

Charles Stewart, American barque, from New York via Hobart: 7 cases ink, 69 boxes clocks, 6 packages containing 24 boxes clocks, 4028 cases kerosine [sic] oil, 2 cases and 1 box springs, 7 cases leather, 21 barrels and 23 cases whiting, 4 boxes and 18 cases paint, 75 cases turpentine, 8 cases grease, 3 cases presses, 2 cases axle grease, 27 cases tools, 20 packages woodware, 23 packages sundries, 3000 staves, 2 cases machinery, 20 cases handles, 4 cases and 5 casks hardware, 1000 boxes prepared corn, 6 cases bolts, 264 cases chairs, 350 cases corn-flour,

10 cases scales, 30 cases blacking, 10 cases polish, 1 case pumps, 1 case knobs, 25 packages glassware, 2 cases and 1 package agricultural implements, 2 boxes 100 quarter-barrels and 30 half-barrels apples, 1 box and 1 crate stoves, 5 half-barrels codfish, 50 cases canned fruits, 16 cases handles, 7 packages carriages, 38 cases carriage ware, 75 pieces plank, 26 loose oars, 1 bundles oars, 12 shellers, 2 packages and 2 cases cornshellers, 50 packages washboards, 36 kegs ink, 90 cases axes, 5 cases hatchets, 25 cases picks, 20 cases half-axes, 4 cases lath hatchets, 10 cases shoe pegs, 32 cases glass, 10 barrels plaster, 15 cases axe handles, 3 cases adze handles, 6 cases organs, 3 cases hammers, 100 barrels resin, 2 cases spades, 4 cases braces, 4 casks lanterns, 3 cases mattresses, 2 cases wrenches, 8 cases saws, 11 cases shovels, 2 cases hay forks, 5 cases stone, 4 cases rollers, 2 cases tacks, 6 cases chimneys, 3 cases pain-killer, 7 cases effects, 2187 cases jams, 50 bags onions, 130 cases fruit, 548 bags bark, 25 cases tobacco, and a quantity of cargo not described on the manifest.

After this cargo had been discharged, evidently no new cargo had been arranged for the bark to pick up in Brisbane, for on July 4 or 5, probably acting on instructions from the Bangor owners or the New York agent, Captain Atwood and Hattie began a long, lonely, dull sail in ballast[G] across the Pacific to Valparaiso, Chile. Thence they sailed up the Western coast of South America to the island of Lobos de Afuera off the Peruvian coast to load guano (coagulated bird droppings) for sale as fertilizer in Spain. Having been loaded with 885 tons of guano (probably not the most sweet-smelling of cargoes!) mined from the huge deposits accumulated over the centuries on the island, the bark recrossed the Pacific to Gilbraltar. There Captain Atwood received instructions to take the guano, much prized in Europe, to Barcelona, where it was unloaded.

Where to then? Evidently again no suitable local cargo had been lined up for the *Charles Stewart*, and so the vessel was sent, again in ballast, through the Mediterranean to Trapani, Sicily, where at the famous salt works she took on a cargo of salt for Rockland, Maine. She arrived at Rockland on June 11 and two days later began off-loading the salt at North Haven harbor, a center of the Maine fishing industry.

The cargoes carried by the *Charles Stewart* on her succeeding voyages even more closely reflected the goods in which the Stewarts normally dealt. For instance, on Hattie's second voyage, which started from Bangor on October 21, 1884, the bark carried orange box shooks to the orange growers of Messina, Sicily. What she brought from Sicily to Boston on her return trip was probably fruit. Boston would have been an apt market for Sicilian oranges and lemons.

In 1885, in a passage that I have quoted above from the last page of his meteorological log of his 1884 voyage to Liverpool, Captain Atwood laments bitterly that it is becoming harder and harder for sailing vessels to procure varied commercial cargoes. Steamships particularly are forcing them out. There are too many vessels for the amount of cargo to be carried. Under this pressure, as the 1880s progressed toward their close, sailing vessels were increasingly forced to carry bulk cargoes for which the element of speed was less important. Hence hauling of coal to Bangor both from the coal ports in the American

South and from Scotland became a principal business of the Stewarts.

That 1884 voyage exactly fits the new situation. Leaving Bangor on July 27, 1884, the *Charles Stewart* arrived at Glasgow, or more likely its principal seaport Greenock, on August 13. On the return trip the bark left Greenock on September 11 and arrived back on October 4—a 75-day round trip from Bangor to Bangor. What she carried to Scotland is not indicated. Perhaps it was Maine lumber or spoolwood, or perhaps she was forced to sail in ballast. But on her return she brought 600 tons of coal loaded either at Greenock, which had excellent rail connections, or more likely Bowling, a small Clydeside port which was the transshipment point between sea-going vessels and the canal boats on the Forth and Clyde canal. It is interesting and important to note that the meteorological log specifically states that the coal was not consigned by a specific seller to a specific buyer but was bought on the bark's, that is the Stewarts', own account. They were not in this instance mere commission agents but were themselves buying for import and, presumably, sale.

The last two voyages of the *Charles Stewart*, those under her new master Johnson Grant after Atwood had retired, were also to Scotland for coal and followed a similar pattern. On the second of these, the bark's last voyage, she was returning from Greenock with a cargo of coal when she struck on Ragged Island. This time, however, the coal was not owned by the Stewarts; it had already been consigned to the Maine Central Railroad. Hence, though they lost the bark, they were not financially responsible for the loss of the coal. A small blessing indeed in comparison to the loss of the vessel itself!

OFFICERS AND CREW

Fortunately the crew list of the *Charles Stewart* on its departure from New York in 1883 with Hattie Atwood on board has been preserved in the National Archives. It is reproduced in slightly abbreviated form on the following page. The ship's company of the bark resembles that of the average American merchant sailing vessel of the second half of the nineteenth century. The captain and mates were Americans, but the bulk of the crew were not. Note that, including the captain, the entire ship's company numbered only 11. If the captain and officers and cook are excluded, there are only 7 regular seamen. No wonder that in emergencies when the vessel was continually changing from tack to tack in a narrow, dangerous channel the crew must have heartily welcomed Hattie's assistance when she took the wheel, freeing an additional seaman for sounding or trimming the yards.

The 34-year-old first mate Horace C. Whitmore was born in Hampden in 1849. He had served as a private in the Civil War.[45] He was a member of the Hampden Congregational Church, having been received into full fellowship on March 2, 1873. On October 30, 1876, he had married in Hampden Catherine R. Sewall, who, Hattie says in her book, had been her Sunday School teacher. By the time of Hattie's second voyage in 1884-85 he had left the *Charles Stewart* to become captain of another T. J. Stewart & Company vessel, the brig *Harry Stewart*[v]. Indeed, two times during 1886 the *Bangor Whig and Courier* reports the arrival in Bangor of that brig with Whitmore as master. The first arrival was from Grenada, cargo unspecified; the second arrival was from Newport News with a cargo of coal for the Lincoln Pulp Mill in Lincoln, Maine, just up the Penobscot River from Bangor. Since he is listed on the Hampden vot-

CREW LIST.

Office of the U. S. SHIP

Port of

LIST OF

Composing the Crew of the *Bark Cha*

N. Atwood is Master

NAMES.	PLACES OF BIRTH.	PLACES OF RESIDENCE.
...s C. Whitm...	Maine	
...ik Florin	New York	
...n Samuel	China	
...ph Mc Gregor	Scotland	
...rie Anderson	Sweden	New York
...ge Thomas	France	
...ma Nainey	Sweden	
...chin Mott	Germany	
...	England	
...iam Lewis	Maine	

Crew list of the bark, 'Charles Stewart'.

178

PERSONS

Stewart" of New York whereof
nd for *Hobart Town*

COUNTRY OR SUBJECTS.	AGE.	HEIGHT. FEET.	INCHES.	COMPLEXION.	HAIR.	EYES.
States	34	5	6	Light	Brown	Blue
"	30	5	4	"	"	"
.a.	37	5	5	Yellow	Black	Black
Britain	32	5	6	Light	Brown	Blue
den	23	5	5	"	"	"
ice	25	5	5	"	"	"
den	36	5	6	"	"	"
u auy	25	5	5	"	"	"
Britain	32	5	6	Black	Curly	Black
d States	20	5	5	Light	Brown	Blue

ing lists up to 1898, Whitmore evidently remained a citizen of that town. In 1904 he is listed, as a retired sea captain in the area would be apt to be, as a farmer. Both he and his wife died in 1929 and are buried in the Locust Grove Cemetery, where Horace Atwood and his wife also lie. Hattie describes him as red-headed with a ruddy complexion.

According to the crew list the second mate Fredrik Florin was born in New York and a citizen of the United States. Hattie, however, calls him a Swede, but she probably means only that he was of recent Swedish descent, looked the part, and perhaps spoke with a Swedish accent. On Hattie's second voyage the mate was a Mr. Ellis of Hampden. Of him I have found no record.

Except for one, all members of the crew of the *Charles Stewart* were foreigners. Two were born in Sweden, and one each in Scotland, England, Germany, and China. One—the Englishman William Bender—was black. The cook and steward John Samuel, usually called Ah Sam, was Chinese. Cooks on American vessels of the era were frequently non-white. The one American, Willie Lewis, was a Hampden boy about Hattie's age. She must have known him well. Though, probably for legal reasons, he listed himself as 20, he was really only 16. His subsequent career was sadly brief. His tombstone in Locust Grove Cemetery states that he was only 22 when he died in Santo Domingo in the West Indies in December, 1888. Tom Hainey, his leg broken in an accident in a violent storm, was left in the hospital in Hobart and so did not return with the bark.[46] According to Hattie's account, only four of the original crew returned with the vessel to the United States. On Hattie's second voyage, just after the *Charles Stewart* left Barcelona for the voyage home, a stowaway was found aboard. He was a young Swiss artist named Charles Bieri, a brother of one of the members of the crew, who was eager to get to the United States. He was allowed to stay on board. Perhaps in gratitude for his passage he later gave Hattie several of his paintings, which at the time of her writing she had hanging on the walls of her home. One of these is the portrait of the *Charles Stewart* reproduced in this edition. Hattie calls him "an artist of no mean talent."

The range of ages of the officers and crew on the *Charles Stewart* was also normal for American vessels of the time: the captain 54 (a little older than usual, but he retired from the open sea the following year); the first mate 34; the second mate 30; and the members of the crew ranging from 16 to 37. It is interesting to note that the two oldest crew members—the Chinese cook at 37 and the black sailor Bender at 32—were both non-white. Probably for them it was more difficult than for the whites to find good jobs ashore when they aged, nor was either apt ever to become an officer. Only a very few non-whites did. They probably had little choice but to keep going to sea. Except for these two, all the crewmen were in or below their twenties.

THE ORIGINAL BOOK

In its original form, *A Trip Around the World* is a small 6-inch by 9-inch volume of 100 pages bound in black cardboard covers. Its cover design (here reproduced) has a nautical flavor. The words of the title are printed to look as if they were made of heavy rope. To the left are spars of a square-rigged vessel; Hattie's name is at the bottom in normal typography. The design is signed "H. Atwood." That could mean that it was drawn by Hattie herself before her marriage, her father Horace Atwood, or possibly her broth-

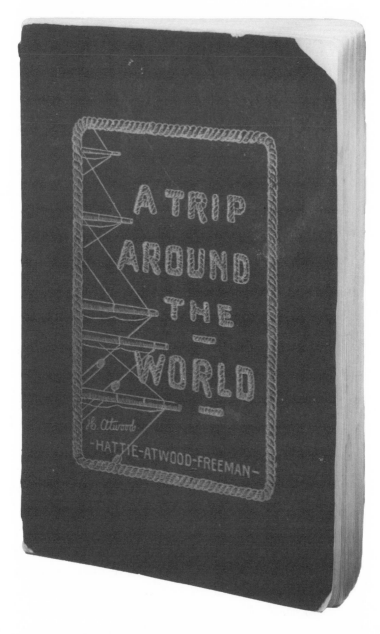

Hattie Atwood's original book. (Author's Collection)

er Horace Welcome Atwood. Over the years the cardboard of the cover has become very brittle.

The frontispiece is a reproduction of the painting of the *Charles Stewart* by the stowaway artist Charles Bieri. The other illustrations in Hattie's book are a reproduction of the photograph of herself that Hattie, as she tells in the book, had taken in Barcelona, and reproductions of photographs of Captain Atwood and mate Whitmore. Unfortunately all were poorly reproduced initially and have now darkened with age. All are reproduced in the present edition, the painting of the bark and the portrait of Hattie from the originals, the others from the copies in the book.

According to its colophon, the book was privately printed in a limited edition from type at the Printery of O.N. Furbush in Bangor, Maine. An advertisement (here reproduced) in the 1907 *Bangor City Directory* places Furbush's press at 20 Harlow Street. After printing, the types were redistributed so that no more copies could be printed—a common practice with a privately printed book.

How many copies were printed it is impossible to say. As far as can be ascertained, only three copies are in public collections. One is in the Maine Collection of the University of Maine in Orono; a second is in the library of the National Maritime Museum in San Francisco. The third copy, which I have used in editing this edition, is in the library of the Norton [Massachusetts] Historical Society. Probably it came to the Society on the death of a member of the Freeman family in Norton. Other extant copies—how many I do not know—are those given by Hattie to other relations and friends such as her niece in Minnesota. Probably the edition was of not more than 50 copies.

The book's Prefatory is dated Norton, Massachusetts, April 26, 1907—Hattie's forty-second birthday.[47]

METEOROLOGICAL LOGS

The phrases and brief sentences printed in italics at the bottoms of some pages of Hattie's text in this edition are quoted verbatim from the official Meteorological Logs that she herself kept for the voyages of the *Charles Stewart* on which she sailed. Both from what she says in her book and from the handwriting and occasional personal remarks in the logs it is clear that Captain Atwood made the keeping of these logs her special job. On the *Charles Stewart*'s July-October, 1884, trip from Bangor to Scotland that Captain Atwood made without Hattie, he himself kept the Meteorological Log. An abstract of Hattie's log for her voyage to Messina, Sicily, and back appears as Appendix I.

The Meteorological Logs were part of an official government program, inspired by the pioneering oceanographic and meteorological work of Matthew Fontaine Maury, to record prevailing wind and weather patterns in all parts of the world where American sailing vessels were apt to go. To captains of ocean-going vessels who would agree to keep them the government offered free special blank log books to be filled out on the voyages and then returned for analysis to the federal meteorological service. From the information thus collected from many ships' logs, meteorological charts and navigation handbooks could be compiled that would be enormously valuable to any sea captain but particularly to the navigators of sailing ships, who needed to know prevailing wind patterns in the areas to which their vessels were bound. Hattie, for instance, when she herself in November, 1884, was navigating the *Charles Stewart* through the Azores, mentions in her own log having consulted the meteorological chart of the area.

The Meteorological Logs were different from the regular ships' logs kept on every vessel, usually by the first mate. As their name implies, they dealt only secondarily with what happened on board; rather, they emphasized and recorded on the two pages allotted for each day, theoretically but not in practice hour by hour, the vessel's latitude and longitude, her course and speed, the direction and character of the winds, any calms, storms, or squalls, any alteration of course, the temperature of the ocean, sightings of other ships or land, even the alterations of sail and course made necessary by the various weather changes—in short anything that when statistically analyzed could assist future navigation.

Unfortunately the log for neither of Hattie's voyages is complete. On her first voyage, shortly after having crossed the Line on the bark's passage from the Lobos Islands to Spain, she broke the thermometer she used for ascertaining water temperatures and, partly at least for that reason, gave up keeping the log on January 29, 1884. She may also have run out of space in her blank log book. On her second voyage, on December 8, 1884, while off the coast of Spain shortly after passing through the Straits of Gibraltar on the way to Messina, she ran out of space and remarks:

My book is finished and I shall think the passage is if we do not get a breeze soon. I have no more log book as I did not receive any before I left.

In addition to technical information, the log books also include occasional general and sometimes personal remarks by the log-keeper. Often these are the most interesting elements in them. For instance, on the long dull voyage from Brisbane to Valparaiso Hattie in her entry for August 19, 1883, vents her exasperation with the loneliness and length of the voyage and wishes, at least fleetingly, that she were back in Hampden with her mother:

PARTICULARS OF T[...]

WIND SCALE.	
Force of Wind, Nautical Scale.	Nautical Designation.
0	Calm.
1	Light airs.
2	Light breezes.
3	Gentle breezes.
4	Moderate breezes.
5	Stiff breezes.
6	Fresh breezes.
7	Very fresh breezes.
8	Moderate gale.
9	Strong gale.
10	Very strong gale.
11	Violent gale.
12	Hurricane; Typhoon; Cyclone.

For a complete definition of this Scale see the Introduction to this Journal.

Midnight squall
at 7 A M Mac[...]
Tasmania N [...]
at 10 South Cape[...]
at 6-30 ,, A.M. the Iron[...]
came to anchor a[...]
without a Pilot[...]
Strong S W win[...]
101 days from [...]

Meteorlogical Logs kept by Hattie Atwood during her voyage around the world. (Author's Collection)

, 18**80**.

ATHER DURING THE DAY.

th rain

N. W. Cape of

4 8 the Heustone

ed Bruni Island

at 10 30 and

bart at 12 Midnight

squall with rain

12

Symbols to be used in recordii
the Weather in the prope

b.—Clear blue sky.
c.—Cloudy weather.
d.—Drizzling, or light rain.
f.—Fog, or foggy weather.
g.—Gloomy, or dark, stormy-l
h.—Hail.
l.—Lightning.
m.—Misty weather.
o.—Overcast.
p.—Passing showers of rain.
q.—Squally weather.
r.—Rainy weather, or continue
s.—Snow, snowy weather, or s
t.—Thunder.
u.—Ugly appearances, or threa
v.—Variable weather.
w.—Wet, or heavy dew.
z.—Hazy.

Symbols to be used in recordi
the Sea in the proper

B.—Broken or irregular sea.
C.—Chopping, short, or cross
G.—Ground swell.

Have not spoken a ship since we left New York or used the signals. Have not seen a sail since we left Brisbane and have had cold wet lonesome weather all the voyage since Brisbane. I want to go home and see marm.

Even in the midst of all the meteorological facts she was recording, Hattie's warm human qualities shine through.

ENDNOTES
Glossary of persons, places, maritime terms and allusions

ALICANTE: seaport on the southeast coast of Spain, not Sicily as Hattie says.

APPLE MARY: unidentified peddler of fruit along piers of New York.

APRIL 26, 1907: Hattie Atwood Freeman's 42nd birthday.

ATWOOD, GEORGE: probably George H. Atwood, who is listed as a sea captain in the Bangor directories from 1877 through 1890. Although it is difficult to know, when an "Atwood" is shown as the master of a vessel, which Atwood it is, he appears to have commanded coastal schooners such as the *Savannah, Vesta, Judge Tenney*, and the brig *Maria W. Norwood* in the 1880s. But there was also a J. H. Atwood, who was in 1879 and 1881 master of the schooner *Charles S. Hazard*. Several of George H.'s vessels are reported in the *Bangor Whig and Courier* as clearing from Bangor to New York.

AUNT BECKIE: Hattie's mother's younger sister Rebecca C. Morey (1849-1927), married to Doane B. Cole.

BARDALONA: in 1884 a small fishing village on the coast north of Barcelona, now a seaside suburb of the city.

BARTHOLDI'S STATUE: the Statue of Liberty, designed by Frederic Bartholdi (1834-1904). Since according to *Webster's Biographical Dictionary* (1953) the statue was not presented until 1885, it is odd that Hattie mentions seeing it in 1883. But preparations for its erection were certainly under way by that date.

BENDER: William Bender, the black member of the bark's crew.

BIERI, CHARLES: painter of the portrait of the *Charles Stewart*, reproduced in this edition. He does not appear in any standard dictionary of painters.

BLAINE, JAMES G. (1830-1893): prominent Maine statesman, congressman, and senator. He won the Republican nomination for president in 1884 but was defeated by Grover Cleveland.

BOCCACIO: *Boccaccio*, a three-act comic operetta in French with music by Franz von Suppae (1819-1895).

BOOBY HATCH: a wooden covering over a companionway hatch.

BOSTON SEMI-WEEKLY JOURNAL (1835-1887): like the *Boston Journal*, of which it was doubtless an offshoot, a mercantile paper which reported the movements of vessels. From it Mrs. Atwood could learn approximately where her husband's vessel had most recently been seen or spoken to.

BOTANICAL GARDENS: The Botanical Gardens in Hobart adjoined the grounds of Government House along the banks of the Derwent.

BOWDITCH: Nathaniel Bowditch (1773-1838) the eminent self-taught American mathematician and astronomer whose *New American Practical Navigator* (1802) was the standard reference book for ocean navigators. In her quotation Hattie is indicating that her book is an edited version (abstract) of the diary or journal which she kept on her voyage. The diary itself has unfortunately disappeared.

BRISBANE: a major Australian seaport, the capital of Queensland. In 1886, three years after Hattie's visit, its population was 32,500.

BUNTING: a thin woolen fabric or a cotton imitation used chiefly for flags.

CAGLIARI: principal seaport and capital of Sardinia situated on the southern coast of the island.

CAPE DE GATA: cape on the southeast coast of Spain near the city of Almeria.

CAPE MORETON LIGHT: a lighthouse on the northeast corner of Moreton Island. It was built of sandstone blocks quarried by convicts exiled from Great Britain.

CAPE PIGEONS: black-and-white petrels, so named because common off the Cape of Good Hope.

CAPE SPARTEL: a cape on the northwest coast of Morocco at the Straits of Gibraltar.

CAPTAIN JOHNSON GRANT: Master of the bark *Charles Stewart* after Horace Atwood had retired.

CASTLE GARDEN: well-known amusement hall at the Battery, at the southern end of Manhattan Island. Under the sponsorship of P.T. Barnum, the famous Swedish singer sang there. It was also, as Hattie notes, an immigrant arrival depot.

CATTING THE ANCHOR: drawing the anchor up to the cathead, a large timber beam fitted with sheaves projecting from each bow of a vessel. The cathead supports the anchor after it has been raised from the water by the chain.

CERETA: misspelling of Ceuta, a seaport in northwest Morocco opposite Gibraltar.

CHARLES STEWART: for a information on the dimensions, history, and owners of the *Charles Stewart* see pages beginning with 161.

CHILDS ART GALLERY: now on Newbury Street, Childs is still one of the best-known and most respected art galleries in Boston.

COMET: the technical name of the comet Hattie saw was P/Pons-Brooks. It was first observed in July, 21, 1812, by J. L. Pons. On September 2, 1883 it was rediscovered by W. R. Brooks. On January 18, 1884, when Hattie first saw it, it would have been extremely bright, the brightest object in the sky. The times of its rising and setting that she gives in her meteorological log entries for January 18, 19, and 26, 1884, are very close to the times that it would have arisen and set in the latitude and longitude where the *Charles Stewart* was on those dates. She was also nearly exact on the degrees about the horizon—ten degrees—that it attained on January 26 at 8:00 p.m. local time. (I am much indebted to Timothy Barker, Professor of Astronomy at Wheaton College, for this information.) Hattie was an accurate observer.

CRIMPS: curls.

DAGO: pejorative slang for Italian, Spanish and Portuguese people.

DECK HOUSE: a shelter of light timber erected on deck for carrying additional cargo.

DEAD RECKONING: calculating a vessel's latitude and longitude without celestial observations but by taking into account her course, her speed, the wind, and any currents that might have affected her progress.

DEALS: planks of pine or fir above seven inches in width and of various lengths exceeding six feet.

DELANO, GEORGE H.: according to the *Maine Register* of 1883 he was the Hampden steamboat agent. He was also the proprietor of the Penobscot House in Hampden.

DIEGO RAMIREZ: one of the southernmost islands in the Tierra del Fuego group. It lies 60 miles southwest of Cape Horn.

DOLDRUMS: a part of the ocean near the Equator characterized by calms and baffling winds.

EVENTIDE of my good father's life: in 1907 Horace Atwood was 76. He would die in 1910 at the age of 81.

FALL RIVER LINE: still in the 1880s the easiest and most comfortable way to travel from Boston to New York. Evening boat trains from Boston took passengers to Fall River, where they boarded steamers, many of them famous for their opulence and comfort, which landed in the morning on the waterfront of downtown New York City.

FATHER'S SISTER: Horace Atwood had two sisters, Helen (sometimes spelled Hellen), born in 1832 or 1833, and Lucinda, born in 1838.

FELUCCA: a narrow, fast, lateen-rigged vessel common in the Mediterranean.

FIGURE OF THE VIRGIN: the Capella del Cristi Risorto, near the monastery of Madonna dell' Annunciata about one and a half miles east of Trapani "contains a statue of the Virgin and Child said to have been brought from Cyprus, to which an immense number of valuable offerings have been made . . . [T]he statue itself is hung with jewels, necklaces, cameos, rings, and watches, &." ("Trapani," *Encylopaedia Britannica*, 11th ed.)

FOX ISLAND[S]: the two Fox Islands are North Haven Island (north Fox Island) and Vinalhaven Island (south Fox Island). To reach the port of

North Haven the bark would have entered the channel between the two islands called the Fox Islands Thorofare.

GANGWAY: a passageway on a ship. The forward gangway on the *Charles Stewart* had a lookout or window from which Hattie could watch the storms as they raged.

"GOAMP": not any bird's real name, but from Hattie's description probably a thin-billed prion or a Hornby's storm-petrel (information courtesy of Professor John Kricher of Wheaton College).

GOUGH'S ISLAND: a rocky outlying island of the Tristan da Cunha group. Lat. 40° 48' S. Long. 12° 4' W.

GREENWOOD CEMETERY: famous cemetery in Brooklyn.

GUANO: compacted bird droppings found in huge quantities on rocky islands off the western coast of South America. Rich in phosphate, guano was mined extensively for fertilizer.

HAMPDEN, MAINE: a small port, agricultural, and commercial town on the west side of the Penobscot River, seven miles below Bangor.

HAMPDEN ACADEMY: a private school or, in nineteenth-century parlance "academy," founded in 1803. It served and still serves also as the Hampden public high school. Since the Academy stood practically in Hattie's back yard, she almost surely attended it.

HOBART: capital of Tasmania. In 1883 when Hattie visited it the island of Tasmania was still an independent British colony, not yet a part of Australia.

HOUSE: the building or superstructure erected on the deck of a vessel often, as here, containing the main cabin. But see also DECK HOUSE.

HOVE TO, HEAVE TO: see below LIE TO, LAY TO.

IMAGE[S]: the images of the Passion carried in procession were those from the Oratorio di San Michele.

IN BALLAST: said of a vessel when she carries no cargo but only iron or stone weights to assist her sailing and steering. Obviously a vessel sailing in ballast was losing money for her owners every day she remained without freight.

IRON POT LIGHT: Iron Pot or Derwent Light at the mouth of the River Derwent that leads up to Hobart.

ISLAND AU HAUT: Isle Au Haut lies at the mouth of Penobscot Bay directly east of Vinalhaven.

JEBEL MUSA: mountain on the Moroccan side of the Straits of Gibraltar, often identified as one of the two Pillars of Hercules, the other being Gibraltar itself.

JORDAN, MARSH & CO.: a major Boston department store, now absorbed by Macy's of New York.

KATE: Catherine Morey (b. February 17, 1844), younger sister to Harriet Atwood and thus Hattie's aunt. Whether or not she was married at the time she showed Hattie some of the sights of Boston is unclear.

LASCARS: East Indian sailors.

LAY TO, LIE TO, HOVE TO, or HEAVE TO: to make the vessel as nearly stationary as possible by turning her into the wind so that she faces the waves and does not roll in the troughs. It is normally accomplished by shortening the leeward sails and holding her helm sharply to leeward.

LINE: the Equator. On her childhood voyage Hattie had crossed it four times. Hence on this voyage she was not obliged to go through the usual ceremony of being initiated by King Neptune.

LIST of souls on board: for the official crew list see pages beginning with 177

LOBOS DE AFUERA: the outermost of a group of bleak, rocky islands of the northern coast of Peru. Guano was particularly plentiful there.

MARGARITE: the tremendously popular opera *Margherita d'Anjou* composed in 1820 by Jacob Meyer Beer [Giacomo Meyerbeer] (1791-1864).

MATE'S WIFE: Mrs. Horace Whitmore. See below: WHITMORE, Mrs.

MESSINA: a principal city of Sicily located on the Straits of Messina near the northwest corner of the island.

MINISTRY OF LIFE: *The Ministry of Life* was a popular religious book published in 1858 by Maria Louisa Charlesworth (1819-1880). Between 1858 and 1870 it appeared in at least seven editions.

MORETON BAY: the large body of water between mainland Australia and Moreton Island. A ship must cross it in order to reach Brisbane.

MOREY, WILLIE: William Morey, Jr. (1864-1916): son of Hattie's maternal uncle William Morey. On April 14, 1884, he had filed in Hampden his intention of marriage with Angie Chapman of Orono, Maine.

MOUNT DESERT ROCK: a small rocky islet only 12 feet above sea level 26 miles off Mount Desert Island. It was known for its lighthouse originally built in 1829. Though the islet posed no important hazard, the light was very useful for navigational purposes. Seamen took their bearings from it. (Charles B. McLane with Carol Evarts McLane, *Islands of the Mid-Maine Coast* [Falmouth, Maine: Kennebec River Press, 1989], II, 99-101).

MUSEUM: P.T. Barnum's American Museum was one of the most popular attractions ever established in New York. It was in its heyday in 1883. Hattie may well have seen there the famous dwarf Tom Thumb and the noted elephant Jumbo. The Museum was filled with curiosities of all kinds.

NORTH HAVEN: a large island near the mouth of Penobscot Bay near Vinalhaven.

PASSION HOUSE: the Oratory of San Michele, which contains seveteenth- or eighteenth-century colored wooden groups carved by native Trapani workmen representing scenes from the Passion. They were intended to be carried in procession.

PICTURES: one of the pictures Hattie had taken in Barcelona was the portrait of herself reproduced in this edition. Mrs. Eloise Valentine Freeman Smith of Pawcatuck, Connecticut, owns the original.

PLUM DUFF: a stiff flour pudding containing raisins. It is boiled in a bag. It was a favorite seaman's dish.

POLONAISE: a woman's garment consisting of a waist and drapery in one piece worn over a separate skirt.

POOP DECK: that section of the deck of a vessel aft of the mizzen mast, often raised.

OLD SONG: "Life on the Ocean Wave" was the most famous poem written by the Boston author and journalist Epes Sargent (1813-1880). It was published in 1847 in *Songs of the Sea and Other Poems.*

RAGGED ISLAND: see Rugged Island below.

RAMBLA: still Barcelona's best-known boulevard and promenade: broad, with trees in the middle and shops on both sides–the place to see and be seen–thronged day and night.

RIVER leading up to Brisbane: the Brisbane River. Though a small river, it is navigable by large ships the 25 miles from Moreton Bay to the city.

ROCKLAND: a major Maine port on the south shore of Penobscot Bay near its mouth.

ROSS, WALTER: listed in the 1884 *Bangor Directory* as a clerk in the office of Ross and Howell, proprietors of towboats. Evidently he also played a more active role as captain of a tugboat.

RUGGED ISLAND: error for Ragged Island, a small rocky, ledge- surrounded island seaward of Matinicus Island approximately 20 miles into the Atlantic in the outermost part of Penobscot Bay. Its reefs made it a dangerous place for ships (Samuel Adams Drake, *The Pine-Tree Coast* [Boston, 1891], 249).

SADDLEBACK ROCK LIGHT: lighthouse on Saddleback Ledge slightly southeast of Vinalhaven Island in Penobscot Bay.

City of SAINT JULIAN: San Giuliano, the ancient city of Eryx over Trapani, with huge Cyclopean walls, and crooked, narrow streets. According to Vergil, it was founded by Aeneas on his voyage from Troy as a Trojan city. It contains the remains of the ancient temple of Venus Erycina. On its heights is also a later, perhaps partly Carthaginian castle covered in Hattie's time with ivy. The road up to it from Trapani was winding, steep, and long.

SAINT MARIA or SAINT MARY: Santa Maria, most southeasterly of the Azores Islands.

SAINT PAUL DE LOANDA: Hattie's error for Saint Paul Rocks, a group of uninhabited volcanic rocks in the Atlantic almost on the Equator 600 miles northeast of Natal, Brazil (1°N, 29°15'W). St. Paul de Loanda is a seaport in Angola, Africa.

SAINT ROQUE: San Roque, a small city six miles from Gibraltar founded by Spaniards who emigrated in a body to Spain when the British took Gibraltar.

SALT PANS: "There are also large salt-pans to the south of the city, extending along the coast as far as Marsala, which produce about 200,000 tons of salt annually," more than half of which is exported to Norway, Sweden, Canada, and the United States. "The numerous wind-mills are used for grinding the salt" ("Trapani," *Encyclopaedia Britannica*, 11th ed.). For a description of the salt works see Arthur Stanley Riggs, *Vistas in Sicily* (New York, 1912), 243.

SHOE PEG: a small pin of tough wood used in securing the uppers to the sole-leather or in building up the heel.

SMITH, Samuel Francis (1808-1895): author of "My Country 'Tis of Thee" and editor in 1843 of *The Psalmist*, for 30 years the widely used Baptist hymn book.

SOUNDING: to take a sounding is to drop the lead to determine how deep the water is.

SOUNDS: the swimming bladder of a fish. Some fishes' sounds are esteemed as food. That of the cod when fried tastes something like a fried oyster.

SOUTH STREET: in 1883 the principal waterfront street bordering New York harbor on the east side of lower Manhattan. Pier 6 was far down toward the Battery.

SOUTHERN CROSS: a constellation in the Southern Hemisphere made especially striking by four exceptionally bright stars arranged in the shape of a Latin cross

SPOOLWOOD: spoolwood is lumber from which wooden spools are made. It was shipped in the form of spool bars to the great thread factories of Scotland and England.

STEM AND STERN: the stem or foremost timber of one vessel is fastened to the stern of the second.

Mr. STEWART: Thomas Jefferson Stewart. See Background and Notes, page 166 and following pages.

STORM HOUSE: it is not entirely clear what Hattie means. A storm house is usually a temporary structure erected to protect workmen in stormy weather. Where on the vessel this was and why it had a window are unclear unless it had been erected to protect the steersman from the hurricane then raging. It may well, however, be the same as the "look out in the forward gangway" she mentions earlier, "where," she says, "I have witnessed many a raging storm." See GANGWAY above.

SURVEY: an official examination to determine the condition of a vessel. Ships were obliged to have periodic surveys. In this case the crew had evidently mutinied because of the *National Eagle*'s potentially dangerous condition.

TALMAGE, Thomas De Witt (1832-1902): Brooklyn Presbyterian minister who received national attention for his sensational preaching style. The Brooklyn Tabernacle where Hattie went to hear him was built especially for him.

TARAPINA: error for Trapani.

TARIFA: a cape and seaport in Spain just west of the Straits of Gibraltar. As Hattie notices, there was a strongly fortified citadel in the harbor and also a lighthouse on the cape.

TASMAN HEAD: the south point of Bruny Island off the southeast coast of Tasmania.

TASMAN RIVER: apparently a mistake for Derwent River. Coming in from the open sea, the *Charles Stewart* would first see Cape Bruny Light off the southern end of Bruny Island, pass Tasman Head, then sail into Storm Bay. At Iron Pot Light she would enter the Derwent River, up which Hobart is located.

TOP GALLANT FORECASTLE: an elevated deck in the bow of a vessel.

TRAPANI: in 1883 an important seaport on the west coast of Sicily. It imported timber and coal, both of which items were important to T. J. Stewart & Company's business, and exported salt, again a commodity in which the firm dealt and which the *Charles Stewart* on Hattie's voyage carried back to Maine.

TRY WORKS: after the blubber (oil-filled outer layer) of a whale had been stripped from its body ("cutting in"), it was thoroughly cooked in huge iron pots on the deck of the whaler until all the oil was "tried out" of it for storage in casks.

TUNNEL: a funnel or other cone-shaped device for pouring.

UNDER ORDERS: that is, the *Charles Stewart* was not a free agent but was obliged to put in at Gibraltar to pick up orders from her owners or New York agent as to where to discharge her cargo. In this case she was directed to go to Barcelona.

WEAR SHIP: a maneuver by which a vessel is brought to the other tack by causing it to swing around before the wind.

WHITMORE, HORACE C.: For information on First Mate Whitmore see Officers and Crew of Background and Notes.

WHITMORE, Mrs.: the mate's wife and Hattie's Sunday School teacher, Katherine R. (Sewall) Whitmore (1852-1929).

LIST OF VESSELS
Met by the bark *Charles Stewart* or mentioned in the background and notes[48]

Amicitia. Of Bergen. P. Riemens, master. Iron screw steamer. Built 1883 in Bergen. 529 tons. Dimensions 172/26/14. Owned O.O. Bergh.

Blandina Dudley. Of Boston. Atwood, master 1856 to 1862 or 1863. Built 1856 in Newburyport. Medium clipper. Oak. Copper and iron fastenings. 850 tons. Owners Mosley and Goreld. Atwood was the first master.

Castlefond. Probably misprint for *Castleford* here described. Of Liverpool.
Screw steamer. Built 1883 in Sunderland. 2006 tons. Dimensions
321/40/29. Owned Castleford S.S.

Ceto. Of London. G. Tucker, master. Iron screw steamer. Built 1878 in
Stockton. 742 tons. Dimensions 215/29/16. Owned H. Cloake.

Charles Stewart. See Background and Notes.

Collingwood. Of London. H. N. Forbes, master. Ship. Built 1872 in
Aberdeen. 1011 tons. Dimensions 211/34/21. Owned Devitt and Moore of
London. Or of Newcastle. Rule, master. Screw steamer. Built 1876 in
Newcastle. 561 tons. Dimensions 215/29/115. Owned by R. Rowe.

Esther Roy. Of Maitland, N.S. Ship. Built 1877 in Maitland by Frieze and
Roy. 1560 tons. Dimensions 219/41/24. Sold to Italians [for salt trade?].

Eudora. Of Yarmouth, N.S. Bark. Built 1882 in Maccan, N.S. by John
O'Brien. 1110 tons. Dimensions 185/38/22. Or of Plymouth (England?). G.
Geach, master. Bark. Built 1863 in Quebec. 416 tons. Dimensions 137/29/
17. Owned P. Wilson of Plymouth. Or of London. G. Cripsey, master. Built
1864 in Montrose. 802 tons. Dimensions 130/25/14. Owned P. Croft.

Eyvor. Of Boston. Barkentine. Built 1874 in Belfast, Maine. 540 tons.
Dimensions 138/32/18.

Garibaldi. Of New York. Ship. Atwood master 1868-1869. Built 1860 Mystic,
Connecticut, by Maxson, Fish & Co. Medium clipper. Oak. Copper and iron
fastenings. 1433 tons. Draft 22. Three decks. Dimensions 182/37/28.
Original owner Calvin Adams. Later owned Hawes and Crowell of Boston.
"The *Garibaldi* was one of the prominent members of the early California
grain fleet and, although she made several voyages in the Far East Trade,
most of her life was spent in trade between San Francisco, New York and
Liverpool. She was an unusually fast sailer. Among the commanders of the
Garibaldi was Captain Horace Atwood who had previously been master of
the *Blandina Dudley* and in later years of the ship *Tennyson*, both of which
were employed in the East India trade." Toward the end of her career she
was under German ownership and operated in the transatlantic trade.
(Matthews, II, 130-131. See also Fairburn,[v], 2858-2860).

Gem of the Ocean. Of Boston. Ship. Built 1852 Medford by Hayden &
Cudworth for William Lincoln of Boston. Used in lumber, ice, gold, and

East India and Australia trade. 702 tons. Dimensions 152/31/20. Billet head. Wrecked 1879 on Vancouver Island. (See Matthews; Hall Gleason, *Old Ships and Ship-Building Days of Medford 1630-1873* [West Medford, 1936]) and Fairburn, *Merchant Sail*, Vol. III. Famous for swift passages. On one of her voyages Horace Atwood was mate.

Harry Stewart. Of Bangor, Maine. Brig. Built September, 1867, in Bangor. 285 tons. Dimensions 113.5/28/14.6. Owned Thomas J. Stewart.

Innerwick. Of Pictou. Bark. Built 1882 in River John, N.S. by J. Kitchin. 1220 tons. Dimensions 194/38/22. Sold to Italians 1905. Wrecked November, 1913.

John C. Potter. Of Searsport, Maine. Ship. Built 1869 in Searsport. 1244 tons. Dimensions 190/36/24.

Karman. Of Helsingborg, Sweden. P. Nordfelt, master. Schooner. Built 1879 in Helsingborg. 296 tons. Dimensions (in meters) 32/7/4. Owned C. Sylvan.

Mercidita. Of Boston. Barkentine. Built 1861 in New York, N.Y. 814 tons. Dimensions 178/29/20.

Montana. Of Newburyport. Ship. Atwood master 1872. Built November, 1865 in Newburyport. Oak and chestnut. Single bottom. Iron and copper fastenings. 1269 tons. Draft 21. Owned J. Currier and others. Employed in ice trade. Burnt and lost under Atwood near St. Paul Island in the Indian Ocean. (See also *Ship Registers of the District of Newburyport* 1789-1870, compiled from the Newburyport Custom House Records on deposit in the Essex Institute [Salem, Massachusetts: Essex Institute, 1937], 156).

National Eagle. Of New York. Medium clipper. Built 1852 in Medford, Mass. by Joshua T. Foster for Fisher and Co. of Boston. 996 tons. Dimensions 179/36/24. Owned Fisher and Company. Her first master was Knott Pedrick of Marblehead. In 1854 she made the Boston to San Francisco run in 134 days. On March 22, 1884—just 29 days after Hattie saw her in Gibraltar harbor—she became a total loss when on a voyage to Fiume, Austria, from New York. She was driven ashore near Bari on the Adriatic coast of Italy. For a picture and further information see *Old Sailing Ships of New England* (Boston: Charles E. Lauriat Co., 1923), 74-75, and Hall Gleason, *Old Ships and Ship-Building Days of Medford, 1630-1873* (West Medford, Massachusetts, 1936). That the crew had mutinied and that Captain Atwood makes a survey of the ship indicate that she was in bad condition.

Olive Thurlow. Of New York. Bark. Built 1876 in Calais, Maine. 660 tons. Dimensions 149/32/17.

Patriarch. Of Aberdeen. H. Plater, master. Iron steamer. Built 1869 in Aberdeen by W. Hood and Co. 1338 tons. Dimensions 221/38/22. Owned by G. Thompson and Co.

Souvenir. Of Bristol, England. W. Day, master. Built 1875 in Norway. 482 tons. Dimensions 142/29/17. Owned E.C. Cummings and R.H. Martin, or of Yarmouth, N.S. Bark. Built 1876 in Belliveau's Cove, N.S. by W. D. Lovitt Fleet. 828 tons. Dimensions 164.7/34.5/20. In March, 1884 abandoned in North Atlantic. Picked up and towed into Flores Island in the Azores.

Tennyson. Of Newburyport. Ship. Atwood, master 1870-1871. Built Newburyport May, 1865, by John Currier. Oak. Copper and iron fastenings. 1247 tons. Draft 20. Owners William Graves & Co., Newburyport merchants "extensively engaged in trade with India." Cost more money to build than any other ship built there up to that time. Employed largely in trade from Liverpool to San Francisco and the Far East, especially India, though she also visited Singapore and Hong Kong, from the latter of which on one voyage she brought 565 coolie passengers to San Francisco. According to Matthews, after her maiden voyage she was always under the command of Capt. Alexander Graves "except for one voyage made by a relieving master"—evidently the 1870-1871 voyage under Atwood. On the vessel's next voyage (1872-1873) she carried ice from Boston to Madras and Calcutta. On February 22, 1873, while returning from Calcutta to Boston laden with Indian produce, she encountered a violent hurricane near Mauritius and was lost. Captain Graves and all officers and men except for the second mate and two crewmen went to the bottom (Matthews, VOL II, 329-330). A manuscript note on the back of a photograph at Mystic Seaport, showing the *Tennyson* loading ice in Hampden, reads: "The 'TENNYSON,' Capt. Edward Graves, sailed Jan. 16 for Boston with a cargo of linseed, cutch [a tanning extract derived from mangrove bark], indigo, shellac, cow hides, goat skins, sheepskins, jute, rags, rubber, safflower, bamboo and sundries. Foundered Feb. 22 south of Mauritius. There were only 3 survivors, 2nd mate W.A. Noyes; Clarence L. Putnam, by [boy]; both Americans and J. Davis, seaman, of Germany. They were afloat 8 days on wreckage without food or water. Eighteen of the crew were lost with one passenger, Captain Coney of the

17th Lancers. The survivors were picked up by the British bark *Warren Hastings* [.] The cargo was valued at $325,000. Vessel and freight money were worth $110,000, all heavily insured." Horace Atwood was lucky that he was not the master on that voyage! The quotation gives an excellent example of the kinds of goods which Horace Atwood must have brought back from his many voyages over many years in the East India trade. On this her last voyage the *Tennyson* may well have transported to India ice, from Hampden, Maine, on which Hattie and her brothers and sisters might have skated.

Victoria. Of Boston. Ship. Atwood, master 1873-1878. Built 1873 Newburyport. Oak and yellow pine. Copper and iron fastenings. 2 decks. 1348 tons. Draft 22. Dimensions 205/38/24. Medium clipper. Owned E. S. Mosely & Co., later Mosely & Currier.

Yuba. Of Pictou, N.S. Bark. Built 1873 in River John, N.S. by C. McLennon. 879 tons. Dimensions 167/35/20. In 1804 registered as of Montreal. Or

Yuca. Of Amlwch, Wales. J. Jones, master. Built 1860 in Workington, England. 483 tons. Dimensions 156/27/18. Owned W. Thomas.

Yula. Probably misprint for *Yuba* or *Yuca*.

APPENDIX I

Summary of the meteorlogical logs of Hattie Atwood's 1884-1885 voyage to Messina, Sicily, and return

Oct. 24, 1884: Sailed this morning from Eagle Island.[G] Passed Saddleback Rock Light[G] at 9:40. At 12 noon Island Au Haut[G] bore 12 miles North Easterly. From noon to 8 PM moderate breeze and pleasant. 2 AM all sail. 4 PM took in royals.

25: Moderate variable breezes at 6 AM. Squall with rain from SW 6 to 8 moderate steady breeze from South. Passing clouds have a sunny appearance. At 8 lightning. Top-gallant sails. Distance run 98 knots. [Hattie writes "knots" for nautical miles.]

26: At 4:30 passed German steamer bound West. 78 knots.

27: Steamer passed bound East. 79 knots.

28: Two barks in sight bound West.

29: 167 knots.

30: Steamer bound east. We see two steamers now to one sailing ship. It won't be long now till sailing ships will be one of the passed and at present not of much account as they do not pay the running expenses. 100 knots.

Nov. 1: Stiff breezes and heavy large swell from SW. Vessel rolling deeply and shipping large quantities of water 183 knots.

4: Today is the presidential election. I hope and pray that James G. Blaine of Maine will be our next *President*. 142 knots.

5: Shipping large quantities of water on deck. 200 knots.

6: 220 knots. [longest 24-hour distance noted in this log]

9: Made Isle of St. Maria^G East distance 40 miles. 60 knots.

10: St. Mary's North distance 12 miles. Town in sight.

12: By the Meteorological Chart it gives as prevailing winds. Southerly for the month so I gave [?] the South side of the Arnel [?] Island the windward side but I find Northeast wind prevailing and very light.

13: Signal Swedish bark from Java 85 days bound to Lisbon.

14: Think I would have done better to keep North of the Islands. I see the Meteorological Chart gives some calm to the North.

16: Light to gentle breezes, passing clouds.

17: Two steamers passed bound southward. Light airs and pleasant. 65 knots. Doldrum clouds all about the horizon.

18: Baffling winds. Several waterspouts about throughout the day.

20: Ship and brig passed bound west. Stiff breezes passing squalls of wind and rain. At 8 wet gloomy squally looking. 75 knots.

21: Choppy sea. 73 knots.

22: Bark in company. Baffling airs all about compass. Dark rainy through the night.

23: At 6 Cape Spartel^G East 40 miles per compass. [Later] Cape Spartel 28 miles distant. 8 PM Spartel Light ENE 15 miles.

24: Squally weather. The wind hauled to Eastward. Put ship about at 10:00 AM. There being strong winds and waterspouts with an increased sea, "hove to" under Cape Spartel. A large fleet blown back through the Straits [of Gibraltar].

25: Moderate gales from the East. Heavy squall weather to Eastward. Heavy clouds rolling in over the land with water spouts. To the West of Spartel clear and pleasant. Standing off and under Spartel with many other vessels. At noon moderating. Out of the whole fleet here we are the only American. How things have changed. Six large steam frigates turned [?] out from the Straights all sail and two four masters. Grand sight and England's glory makes a Yank feel mean when compared with the American.

26: Beating through the Straits. Have worked up to Tarifa^G and put back. Hard squall waterspouts and rain to the Eastward of the Straits and to the Westward of Spartel clear and pleasant weather.
29: Wind come in from SW side [?] of Tarifa^G meets the Easterly gale and forms rains and squalls.
[30]: The morning of the 30 passed Gibralter following up the SW winds that are working into the Mediterranean. Heavy dense clouds overhead.
Dec. 1: The winds last 12 hours baffling from NE to SW, Easterly and Westerly winds fighting for the right of way. We are helping the Westerly winds all we can by working up in the rear and hope we will carry the day for I think the Easterly have had their blow out. Lots of steamers coming and going all the time.
4: Moderate and pleasant throughout. Moderate breeze and pleasant.
7: Everything so fine through this 24 hours I have nothing to say.
8: Moderate calms and clear sea smooth as glass. My book is finished and I shall think the passage is if we do not get a breeze soon. I have no more log book as I did not receive any before I left.

APPENDIX II
Thousand-Mile Race on a Floating Volcano

Telling How Capt. Horace Atwood sailed the Burning Ice Ship *Montana* through the Indian Ocean to St. Paul Island and a Strange Rescue[49]
(L. T. S.)

"That was a great sea story you told in The News the other day," an old timer writes. "You said it was one of the two best you ever heard, that one about the loss of the Ada W. Gould. Now, for the sake of old times, won't you spin the other yarn?"

Well, all right. Here's the other one, as told to us by the late Capt. Horace Atwood of Hampden one day years ago while coming over from Augusta on the train. It's about the burning at sea of a ship laden with—what do you suppose? Oil? No. Coal? No. That ship was full of ice!

Yes! Ice. Capt. Atwood, who had circled the globe many times and faced every sort of peril, declared that his experience in the *Montana* shook him up more than mutinies, hurricanes or anything else in his long life afloat.

SHE WAS A TUDOR SHIP

The *Montana* was one of the Tudor iceships—that is, she was one of the fleet engaged in carrying ice from Boston to India for the once-famous house of Tudor & Co. The Tudors cut and stored great quantities of ice at ponds near Boston, and shipped most of it in their own vessels to Bombay, Rangoon, Calcutta, etc. They had at one time a numerous and splendid fleet, including three ships that were built especially for the trade, called the *Ice King*, the *Iceberg* and the *Iceland*.

Not one of these ice-carrying ships is now afloat, and the fate of the *Montana*, a handsome 1400-ton Newburyport-built half clipper, was similar to that which befell several of the others—burned at sea.

A FLOATING VOLCANO

Although Capt. Atwood had many successful voyages in the ice trade, he always had a dread that one of the floating refrigerators would turn into a volcano under him in mid-ocean, and in the case of the *Montana* his fears were realized. The *Montana* sailed from Boston early in 1872 with a crew of 26 all told, and a full cargo of ice, bound for Rangoon.

She made a good run until well around the Cape of Good Hope, and into the south Indian Ocean, and then, one day, a man was sent to get a tub from the forepeak to catch some fresh water. When the man lifted the hatch a cloud of mingled smoke and steam burst up into his face and he dropped the hatch in dismay and ran aft with the news that the ship was on fire. Capt. Atwood knew well that there was little hope of saving the ship, for an ice ship, like an icehouse, will burn like tinder. The fire, which was caused by spontaneous combustion, was far down among the sawdust dunnage in the cargo, forward, and there was no getting at it directly.

The only thing to do was to try to flood it out. The forepeak hatch was taken off and a line of hose from a powerful deck pump was let down. The men pumped water into the hold all that day and night, but next morning the fire was burning hotter than ever.

Capt. Atwood saw that the end of the *Montana*, and perhaps of all her people, was near at hand, and he looked carefully at his chart. The nearest land was St. Paul Island and that was a thousand miles away. Had the ship not been out of her usual course, having made far to the eastward to take advantage of a wind then blowing from the southwest in that region, she would have been still farther from any land, and Capt. Atwood congratulated himself upon that streak of luck in the midst of disaster.

A RACE WITH DEATH

There was St. Paul Island, and it must be reached if the crew of the *Montana* were to be saved, for in the boats there would not be one chance in a hundred for them. So all sail was cracked on, and the *Montana* showed the best that was in her, while the sailors prayed for luck and the fire raged in the hold.

As the days passed the decks grew hotter and hotter, so that the men, usually barefooted in those latitudes, wore their heaviest boots, while every little while an unusually violent belching of smoke and gas and steam from the hold drove the crew into the rigging to get a breath of fresh air.

While Capt. Atwood and his mates kept their heads and showed no sign of fear or excitement, it was plain that the men forward were on the verge of panic. Several times they had urged that the ship be abandoned, but they were told that it would be suicide to take to the boats so far off the trade courses. This did not quiet them, and there would have been mutiny had Capt. Atwood not acted promptly. "The first man that makes a move toward the boats will get a bullet for his trouble!" the captain said, quietly, and the mutiny died right there.

The holes that had been bored in the deck were now plugged up tight, and the hatches were newly caulked, but the belchings of the volcano came through the seams as through the meshes of a sieve. In the cabins and in the forecastle there was no living, and the cook was driven from his galley. All hands were obliged to stay on deck, or in the rigging, and it was a Godsend that the weather continued fine.

ST. PAUL—JUST IN TIME

As the *Montana* neared St. Paul Island, Capt. Atwood had provisions, water, clothing, instruments and the medicine chest stowed in boats, and the boats were towed astern, that they might be ready in case heavy weather came on when near the island and the crew had to leave her at short notice.

It was on the eighth day that St. Paul was sighted, and on that day a gale came on. The island is nothing but the crater of a volcano, rising a few feet, above the surface of the Indian Ocean, and formed like a great bowl, with fathomless depths all around.

Capt. Atwood knew that there was little holding ground for an anchor and that he would have to go close in shore in order to get any bottom, so he brought her to under the lee of the island, in the face of the gale, and let go the heaviest mudhook he had. It was all so quickly and neatly done that the anchor held and there the *Montana* swung,

The ship 'Montana.' (Peabody Essex Museum, Salem, MA)

under the lee of St. Paul with her hold a seething mass of fire and her crew impatient to leave her.

As she lay there, Capt. Atwood had the men get out more stores and some rigging and sails, and then, having done everything possible for comfort and safety, he gave the order to quit the ship.

LAST OF THE *MONTANA*

The crew had not been on shore many hours when, with a frightful roar, the flames burst through the ship's decks and soared aloft in a red and black torrent, eating up the sails and rigging like chaff. Soon the masts fell, and before night there was nothing left of the ship but her hull under water and a blackened heap of ice in its depths. There was no telling how long the *Montana*'s crew might have to remain on the volcanic isle, for few ships pass that way except under unusual conditions of weather, but they did no worrying, for they had plenty to eat and would not have starved anyway, for the best of food fishes abound in the waters there, while millions of sea fowl frequent the lonely place.

VOLCANO GROWLS

There was little need for shelter, for except in storms the temperature was comfortable. The only thing that caused any uneasiness was the fear that the volcano might resume business, and this fear did not take possession of the men until one day there came an awful rumble, shaking the whole island, which is about one mile one way by two miles the other.

Two of the sailors were sitting on the shore watching out for passing sails, when the quake came, and an immense boulder rolled down from the rim of the volcanic bowl, passing close to the two men and disappearing with a great splash in the sea. "We might as well be roasted as be flattened out with big rocks like that," said the jacks, and they wanted to put to sea at once in the long boat.

When Capt. Atwood landed on St. Paul the first thing he noticed was a flagstaff propped up with boulders, with the tattered remnants of a British Union Jack flying from its weather-worn halliards. He afterward found that a British sloop-of-war had been wrecked on the island, and that this signal had been set up by her people, who, after spending six weeks there, had sent out a boat for help.

Sometime after that another British war vessel came from Singapore and took off the castaways. Upon the flagstaff Capt. Atwood set another signal, the American flag, union down, and then there was nothing to do but wait.

A STRANGE RESCUE

The rescue of the *Montana*'s people came about strangely—they earned their deliverance by preventing the deaths of their deliverers. One night, the sixth they had been upon the island, some of the lookouts were astonished to see a big ship bearing straight for the island, as though her people had not made out the land. In another minute or two she would bring up all standing on the rocky rim of the volcano, and that would be the last of her and her crew, for half a gale was blowing and a smart sea running.

Immediately the *Montana*'s men set up a great shouting and flashing of lights, and at the last instant, as it seemed, the lookout on the on-coming ship saw and heard them. Over went her wheel, and she came up into the wind with a great creaking of yards and slapping of canvas, just clearing the rocks. Capt. Atwood afterward discovered that the master of this ship, which was a Britisher bound from Liverpool to Rangoon, was much addicted to liquor, and that the sailing of the ship devolved altogether upon the mates, neither of whom was much of a navigator.

The *Montana*'s crew were landed at Rangoon, where most of them shipped in other vessels, Capt. Atwood coming home by steamer via Suez.

NOTES ON THE NOTES

1. In 1976 it was torn down in order to make room for a new Academy building.

2. It was not unusual for the child of a sea captain to be named after the vessel in which he or she was born. Nor was it unusual for a captain to take his wife and small children with him on his voyages, though Horace Atwood probably did so more frequently than most captains. The middle name Welcome was given to Hattie's brother Horace because his father, at sea when he was born, wrote back to say that Horace, his first son, was "welcome." Unfortunately the vital records of the Town of Hampden for the 1860s and 70s are missing; the early records of Hampden Academy have disappeared; and the records of the now closed Hampden Congregational Church, which the Atwoods probably attended and whose baptismal or Sunday School records might state the children's ages, cannot be located. The dates of birth of the girls can be deduced from school records, but no such records appear to be extant for the boys. Edward's tombstone, however, indicates that he was born in 1875, and Hattie's niece, Mrs. Henrietta Atwood Briggs, daughter of Horace Welcome Atwood, believes her father was born in 1872. Edward studied at the University of Maine in Orono, but the university has no record of when he was born. He died in 1953. For information on the Atwoods and on Hampden I am much indebted to Mrs. Kathryn Trickey, Ms. Nadine Hoyt, and other members of the Hampden Historical Society, and to Mrs. Henrietta Briggs of Minnesota, who has supplied many of the most colorful details.

3. Very likely it was on this early voyage that, according to family tradition, she was given a gold cross for being the first girl to visit the new mayor. She is wearing it in the portrait of her reproduced in this edition.

4. Why the boys' names do not appear: There may have been a separate list of boy scholars that has not survived, or the boys may have attended Hampden Academy at an earlier age than the girls.

5. *New York Index of Clearances, Foreign*, January 29, 1883: "Flag: American. Rig: bark. Name: *Charles Stewart*. Tons: 603. Crew: 11. Destination: Hobart and B[risbane], Australia."

6. The dates given by Hattie for the departures–January 29 from New York and October 21 from Bangor–differ slightly from those given in the meteorological logs she herself kept on the *Charles Stewart*. The logs say January 30 and October 24. These discrepancies can be explained by the fact that Hattie, basing her book on her diary, gives the days on which the vessel left her berth, while the logs date the voyages from the dates when the bark first came out into the open sea. The passage from Bangor, for instance, out through the islands of Penobscot Bay could well have taken the three days by which Hattie's book and the official logs differ. Dates of arrival at and departure from other ports also slightly differ for the same reason.

7. It may be interesting to compare Hattie's account of one leg of her first voyage–that from New York to Hobart, Tasmania—with another, more technical, but still dramatic narrative of the same passage printed in the May 12, 1883, issue of the *Hobart Mercury* (kindly supplied by the Archives Office of Tasmania) and based on Captain Atwood's and Hattie's comments:

Captain Horace Atwood . . . reports as follows on the passage: Left New York on January 29, with a light N.E. wind; had moderate winds and fine weather till February 22, when the N.E. trades were picked up in 11deg. 16min. N., 37deg. 55min. W. These were carried till the 28th, and the Equator was crossed in 28deg. 48min. W. on March 1. No S.E. trades were experienced at all. Had variable winds till reaching 20deg. S. on the 11th, when she got S. and S.E. winds and carried them down to 38 deg. S. On the 25th she began to encounter heavy westerly gales from N.W. to S.W., with heavy rain and squally weather. These gales commenced in 14deg. W., and were carried down to 129deg.[long.?] E. Ran our easting down between 44deg. and 45deg. S., experiencing westerly gales and thick squally weather throughout. On April 2 had a heavy gale from N.W. At 11:30 that morning she shipped a heavy sea over the stern. It carried away the wheel and everything attached to it, and broke the leg of Thomas Hainey, who was at the wheel; staved in the cabin windows, and flooded the cabin with water. The gale occurred in lat. 42deg. S. and long. 23deg. E., and lasted 24 hours, the ship running all the time. On the 3rd inst in lat. 45deg. S., long. 132deg. E., had a violent gale from S.[?]W. to S.S.E., with a tremendous sea running. The vessel was hove to for 12 hours under mizzen-staysail, and no damage was done to the ship. From there bad winds from S.W. to S.S.E., with heavy rain and thick weather till

*arrival. Made the South-West Cape on Thursday morning at 5 o'clock;
passed the Mewstone at noon; made the South Bruny light at 5 p.m.;
rounded Tasman Head at 6:30 p.m.; abreast of the Pilot station at
8 p.m.; passed the Iron Pot [light] at 10:30 p.m.; and dropped anchor
in the Cove yesterday at 12:45 a.m.; berthing at the new wharf later in
the morning. She is consigned to Messrs. Macfarlane Bros. & Co., and
brings about 305 tons cargo of a miscellaneous description. The
remainder is for Brisbane, whither the vessel proceeds as soon as she
has finished discharging here.*

This was quite a baptism of storm for Hattie, who had not been to
sea since her earliest childhood! A third version of the leg of the voyage between New York and Hobart can be found in the
Meteorological Log that Hattie kept for her father on the passage.

8. Hattie frequently mentions her pleasure in her father's teaching her
    navigation. She learns how to "take the sun to determine the latitude."
    Her father promises her a black silk dress if she can answer a series
    of questions on what he has so far taught her. Because she does so
    well on his quiz, he gives her fifty dollars to buy the dress. She is
    much pleased when she learns how to find the latitude by the
    polar star. Later she says she has been "busy with chronometer and
    rating" in order to determine precisely what the time is. From an
    entry in the Meteorological Log she kept on her second voyage it is
    clear that at times she plotted the course of the bark. She remarks
    that, following the advice of the meteorological handbook, in hopes
    of stronger winds, she has taken the *Charles Stewart* around one
    side of an island in the Azores but is sorry that she has done so
    because she found there only light breezes, whereas there was good
    wind on the other side.

9. For information on Edgar Freeman I owe much to George Yelle,
    Benton Keene, Sr., and other members of the Norton Historical
    Society. Harry Burbank has kindly supplied invaluable copies of
    census records and other documents relative to Norton and also
    Hampden.

10. The 1870 federal census of Norton lists a Martha Freeman, wife of
    Henry Freeman, who had been born in Maine. It may be of impor-
    tance too that one of the Cape Cod families that migrated, just as
    the Atwoods did, from Cape Cod to Orrington and Hampden, Maine,

between 1763 and 1825 was a family of Freemans. Freemans and Atwoods may well have known each other even before the deterioration of land on the Cape forced them to seek better farming land in Maine and could possibly have maintained ties to one another. For a fascinating account of this settlement of a Cape Cod "colony" in Orrington and Hampden see James H. Eves. "'The Valley White with Mist': A Cape Cod Colony in Maine, 1770-1820," *Maine Historical Society Quarterly*, 32 (Fall, 1992), 74-107.

11. *Every Day but Sunday: The Romantic Age of New England Industry* (2nd edition, Mansfield, Massachusetts: Mansfield Press, 1956), 44-53. The book is a history of industry in the town of Mansfield.

12. It is interesting that despite living most of her life in Norton and later in Connecticut she always seems to have thought of herself as a Maine person. When she needed a lawyer, she chose a Maine lawyer; when she wanted a printer, she hired a Maine printer.

13. For information on Hattie and Hattie's life after her move to Connecticut I am greatly indebted to descendants of her stepson Charles—Mrs. Eloise Valentine Freeman Smith and Mrs. Marion Leonard Norman of Pawcatuck—and to Hattie's niece, Mrs. Henrietta Atwood Briggs of Arden Hills, Minnesota. Mrs. Smith and Mr. and Mrs. Norman still live within a block of the house on West Broad Street and at this writing still own it. The Normans own the painting of the *Charles Stewart*, and Mrs. Smith has preserved souvenirs that Hattie brought back from her voyages. These include the photographic portrait of herself she had taken in Barcelona (reproduced in this edition), a Spanish *porrón* (a wine bottle with a long spout on its side from which one drinks), and a decorative glass tube on a base filled with layers of different colored guano.

14. While still in Norton she was listed in the 1894 Norton directory as V.N.C. [Norton Vice Commander?] of the Norton Commandery No. 396 of an organization of both men and women identified only as U.O.G.C. It met the second and fourth Saturday of each month in the vestry of the Trinitarian Church. I have been unable to identify what the initials stood for. Merely because it met at the church does not necessarily mean that it was a religious organization; several non-religious groups such as the W.C.T.U. used the Trinitarian vestry as their meeting place.

15. "Pleasant Session Held at Squaw Point," *Bangor Daily Commercial*, August 20, 1920: a report on the address by Edward M. Blanding delivered to a meeting of the Bangor Historical Society on the life and activities of Captain Atwood. Blanding, a Hampden resident, had built his home on land purchased from Atwood.

16. Letter to the editor from Horace's niece Henrietta Atwood Briggs.

17. Such was probably the case particularly in the Hampden-Orrington area. In the article "The Valley White with Mist': A Cape Cod Colony in Maine" cited above, Eves emphasizes that the Cape Cod "colonists" who came to that region had been farmers on the Cape, not seamen or fishermen, and left it only when the soil became so thin they could no longer make a living from the land. Thus when they came to Maine, they still thought of themselves primarily as agriculturists even when many of them became lifelong seamen as Horace Atwood did. Horace himself, of course, owned a large farm in Hampden.

18. Richard Morey Sherman, "A Hampden, Maine, Morey Family," *Downeast Ancestry*, XIV (August-September, 1990).

19. In Hattie's handwriting on the back of a picture of the *Gem of the Ocean* in the possession of Marion Norman of Pawcatuck is written: "My father was mate of her."

20. The events of this voyage are recounted by a passenger aboard the *Blandina Dudley*, Thomas Kinnicut, Jr. of Worcester, Massachusetts, whose journal of his trip is in the library of Mystic Seaport. In general, in the absence of other sources of information, my dating of the various commands which Atwood held is based on the names of each ship's master noted in the annual volumes of the *Record of American Shipping* issued by the American Shipmasters Association, later called the *American Bureau of Shipping; American Lloyd's Register of American and Foreign Shipping*; and in two cases on the *New-York Marine Register of American Ships*. In some instances when I have been unable to consult any one of these registers, I have deduced dates from what other evidence is available. In regard to the *Blandina Dudley*, for instance, no register is available for either 1859 or 1860. I have assumed that Atwood was master in those years, since he was master 1856-58 and 1861-63. It must be noted,

however, that though each register purports to show who was captain on January 1 of each year, the information must have been often compiled much earlier. Even on publication the registers may sometimes have been up to six months out of date on any specific vessel.

21. Atwood appears to have relinquished the command of the *Blandina Dudley* sometime in 1863. What he was doing from 1864 to 1868, when he became master of the *Garibaldi,* is unclear. The annual registers do not list him as master of either of those two vessels. According to a deed in the Penobscot County Registry of Deeds, in 1864 he bought a livery stable in Hampden, but it is difficult to envision this vigorous and experienced master of vessels being content with hiring out spavined hacks and broken-down shays for shopping trips to Rockland or picnic jaunts to Winterport.

22. For my information on the California grain trade I am indebted to Professor Briton Busch of Colgate University and to James H. Hitchman, *A Maritime History of the Pacific Coast 1540-1980* (Lanham, Maryland.: University Press of America, 1990), 23-34. In the 1860s and 1870s California's greatest export crop was grain. Wheat production rose to a $30,000,000 business. In the period from 1880 to 1884, more than 1500 sailing vessels carried grain to Great Britain. Three-quarters of these sailed from San Francisco. Trade to California involved liquor, tools, and cordage. As early as the 1850s more than 100 clippers a year entered San Francisco Bay. The fact that vessels engaged in the grain trade sometimes brought paving stones, some still identifiable in city streets, to San Francisco I owe to the courtesy of William Koiman of the Library of the National Maritime Museum in San Francisco.

23. Deed of James A. Swett to Horace Atwood, June 23, 1869. James Swett was the son of Benjamin Swett, whose wife was Mehitable Atwood, Horace's aunt. Benjamin (1767-1854) had bought the farm in 1793 when he came to Hampden from Wellfleet, Massachusetts, where he had been born in 1767. In 1794 he married Joanna Atwood of that town, daughter of Ebenezer Atwood. The year after her death in 1801 he married Mehitable Atwood of Orrington, Maine, daughter of Jesse Atwood and therefore Horace Atwood's aunt. The Atwoods and the Swetts seem to have come to Maine from Massachusetts together in the migration of Cape Codders to Maine described by

Eves in his "Valley White with Mist" article cited above. Eves names Jesse Atwood as one of the "colonists." Benjamin and Mehitable had twelve children, all of whom were living in 1833. James A. Swett (born 1808) was their fourth child. He evidently inherited the farm in 1854. (Information on the Swett genealogy kindly sent me by Nadine Hoyt of the Hampden Historical Society). For Horace Atwood's acquisition of the property, its extent, and the buildings on it see also "Pleasant Session Held at Squaw Point" cited above. According to this article, the locally famous Battle of Hampden was fought on the Swett farm. On November 6, 1872, Horace deeds over the property in return for "one dollar and love and affection" to his wife Harriet, but does not record the deed. On February 20, 1900, Harriet deeds back the property to Horace for "one dollar with love and affection," but this deed is not recorded until after her death in 1907. The complicated arrangement was probably meant to insure that when one spouse died the other could immediately come into possession of the property.

24. For information on the Tudor Company and the ice trade see the biography of Frederick Tudor (1783-1864) in the *Dictionary of American Biography* and "Ice-Carrying Trade at Sea," *Maritime Monographs and Reports* of the National Maritime Museum, Greenwich, England, No. 49 (1981). Norman E. Borden, Jr., *Dear Sarah: New England Ice to the Orient* (Freeport, Maine: Bond Wheelwright Company, 1966) tells of a voyage in an ice ship. The ice trade from New England to the Orient has been credited with reviving the then faltering New England East India trade.

25. L. T. S., "Thousand-Mile Race on a Floating Volcano," a magazine or newspaper article (periodical, date, and author unknown) in the possession of Mrs. Briggs, from the *Bangor Daily News*. My account of the catastrophe is drawn from that article. The entire article is reprinted as Appendix II of this edition.

26. "Pleasant Session Held at Squaw Point," cited above.

27. That the vessel was not lost is proved by the fact that she appears in the 1879, 1880, and 1881 registers with a Captain Barley as master. In 1882 she disappears from the records.

28. A vessel's Certificate of Registration or Certificate of Enrolment (here

often shortened to "register") was comparable to a modern automobile registration. It listed rig, home port, dimensions, tonnage, owners, current captain, and date and place of construction. It needed to be changed when ownership or home port changed. Six of the *Charles Stewart's* registers are preserved in the National Archives:

Temporary Register No. 3 issued November 6, 1877, at Belfast, Maine, Custom House on the basis of the Master Carpenter's and Surveyor's certificates

Temporary Enrolment No. 54 issued May 10, 1878, at the Gloucester, Massachusetts, Custom House

Permanent Register No. 560 issued June 5, 1878, at the New York Custom House

Permanent Register No. 129 issued November 6, 1882, at the New York Custom House

Temporary Certificate of Enrolment No. 170 issued April 1, 1886, at the Boston Custom House

Temporary Registration No. 21 issued May 21, 1885, at the Bangor Custom House

Whenever a new register was issued, an official form had to be made out certifying that the old one had been surrendered. These too have been preserved.

29. Information from Henrietta Atwood Briggs.

30. Information courtesy of the Maine Maritime Museum. Atwood's colleague was responsible for inspecting steamboat boilers.

31. Information on appointments courtesy of the Maine State Archives. The Board acted under the terms of Chapter 172 of Maine legislation. For information on his retirement from his post and his life thereafter see "Pleasant Session at Squaw Point."

32. His will, dated August 18, 1906, (just after the death of his wife Harriet), and probated January 21, 1910, stipulated that all his real

estate in Hampden and all his personal property was to be divided equally among his children but that a one-third share in the Sebecco Lake House, a boarding house or hotel that he owned on Sebec Lake in Sebec County, Maine, should go to his son Horace Welcome Atwood with the privilege of buying the other two-thirds from the other heirs.

33. Inspector's Certificate of Official Number, Tonnage, & issued May 23, 1878, by the Inspector of Customs in New York. The numbers had to be "not less than three inches in length." Application for an official number had been made to the Collector of Customs in Belfast, November 3, 1887, even before the bark's launching.

34. On January 1, 1882, Powers was still listed as master, but by November 6 a new Certificate of Registration lists Atwood.

35. Though in the Epilogue to her book Hattie says that the *Charles Stewart* was lost on its first voyage after her father had given up command, there is evidence that Captain Grant may have made an intermediate voyage to Greenock for coal. For on July 4, 1886, the *Republican Journal* of Belfast noted the arrival in Bangor of the *Charles Stewart*, Grant master, from Greenock. All citations in this chapter to the *Republican Journal* are courtesy of James B. Vickery of Bangor.

36. Doubtless the same tug or another tug owned by the Ross and Hand company as that captained by Walter Ross which came down the Penobscot from Bangor to Rockland carrying Hattie's mother, her two brothers Horace and Edward, Mrs. Whitmore, and Thomas J. Stewart and his daughter Mrs. Vance to greet the *Charles Stewart* on her return on January 12, 1884, from her trip around the world.

37. The best account of Thomas Stewart and his sons is in George Thomas Little, ed., *Genealogical and Family History of the State of Maine* (New York: Lewis Historical Publishing House, 1909), II, 615-617. Two other sources are an obituary in the *Bangor Whig and Courier* of March 7, 1890, and a brief paragraph on him that appeared in 1934 in the *Bangor Daily Commercial.* An obituary of Charles Stewart in the *Bangor Daily News* of January 22 or 23, 1925, (according to Bangor records he died on January 20, 1925) not only

details Charles Stewart's life but also supplies considerably more information on the Stewart firm. I have quoted from it below.

38. He also had a daughter Rosaline, who in 1875 married Lawrence M. Vance of Indianapolis, Indiana. In her book Hattie Atwood mentions the fact that both Mrs. Vance and her father Thomas Stewart were among those who came downriver in the tug from Bangor and Hampden to meet the *Charles Stewart* at her arrival at Rockland in June, 1884.

39. Thomas J. Stewart was a ship broker and commission merchant. Thus he did not manufacture or always even own the products such as shooks and ice that he transported and sold. He made his money from transporting goods in his own vessels or those of other shipowners and by selling those goods, whether shooks or salt or coal or ice, on commission. His son Harry, on the other hand, actually cut lumber, manufactured shooks, and probably actually harvested ice that his father shipped and sold.

40. The August 3, 1886, issue of the *Bangor Whig and Courier* reports that several Italian vessels are in port loading shooks to be shipped by the Stewarts to Mediterranean ports. Especially when American sailing vessels began to diminish in number, it was probably cheaper for the Stewarts to charter Italian vessels than to build and sail their own. They also chartered British steamers. Just how large a fleet the Stewarts themselves owned I have not been able to determine, but vessels named after members of the family appear fairly often in maritime records of the time.

41. Kindly supplied by Ian Pearce, State Archivist of Tasmania.

42. In the book Hattie mentions the organs and tells how she had her father bring one up to the cabin for her use.

43. Courtesy of John Oxley Library of Queensland.

44. Probably barrel staves.

45. Maine State veterans' records show that a Horace C. Whitmore of Bangor enlisted on February 22, 1864, served as a wagoner from March 15, 1864, to February 6, 1865, in Company F of the 31st Maine

Infantry, and was discharged on February 6, 1865. This, however, may not be the future mate of the *Charles Stewart*. On his enlistment this man's age was recorded as 18 and 6 months, his height as 5' 2", and his hair as light. In 1864 the future mate's age would have been only 15, and on the crew list his height is given as 5' 6" and his hair was brown. It may be, of course, that on enlistment the future mate falsified his age and that this was the reason for his discharge after such brief service. At 15 he could have been four inches shorter than he was in 1883, his hair could have darkened from light to brown. Both men had blue eyes.

46. There is a discrepancy between Hattie's enumeration of the crew in her book and the names on the crew list. She mentions Billie, Tom, Henry, George, Bender, and Sam, all of whom can be identified on the list. But her James and Mike cannot, unless they were nicknames for Joseph McGregor and Wilhelm Krott, which seems unlikely. Far more probable is that the *Charles Stewart*, like many other American vessels, lost at least two seaman by desertion and replaced them with two new crew members. Hattie, then, may not necessarily be listing the original crew but the crew after changes had been made. In all probability when Hainey was incapacitated and left in the hospital a new man was signed on in Hobart. Later, in Barcelona, the American consul brought Captain Atwood three men to be shipped.

47. In 1912, five years after the printing of Hattie Atwood's book, appeared a small volume of 172 pages with a confusingly similar title and a surprisingly similar author's name. Published under the *nom de plume* Sydney Ford, it was entitled *Journeying Around the World: A Narrative of Personal Experience* and published by the Grafton Publishing Company of Los Angeles. The author's real name was Henrietta Bennett Freeman, not far different from Hattie's, Hattie Atwood Freeman. But the contents are entirely different. This is the account by an experienced magazine or newspaper writer of her tour in first class in large British ocean liners or cruise ships with all the amenities, including swimming pools. When she goes sightseeing, she goes in a touring car with a chauffeur and a guide. She stays in the best hotels—for instance Shepheard's, in Cairo. She has along numerous large wardrobe trunks and tells her reader how best to pack them. She travels on the best trains, first class. How different from Hattie's simple but adventurous voyages! And how dull in comparison! Even the writing is pedestrian. Henrietta the professional

should have gone to untutored Hattie to find out how to write— and live— vividly and adventurously.

48. Principal Sources: *American Lloyd's Registry of American and Foreign Shipping;* American Bureau of Shipping, *Record of American Shipping; New York Marine Register . . . of American Vessels; Merchant Vessels of the United States;* Frederick C. Matthews, *American Merchant Ships 1850-1900* (Salem, Massachusetts: Marine Research Association); William Wallace, *Record of Canadian Shipping* (London: Hodder and Stoughton, 1930); and William Armstrong Fairburn, *Merchant Sail.* 6 vols., (Center Lovell, Maine: Fairburn Educational Foundation, 1945-55). Other important sources will be specified.

49. Probably from the *Bangor Daily News,* date unknown. Included here through the courtesy of Hattie Atwood's niece, Henrietta Atwood Briggs.